Installation Services for All Groups

Installation Services for All Groups

Amy Bolding

BAKER BOOK HOUSE

Grand Rapids, Michigan 49506

Dedicated to
my mother and father
Reverend and Mrs. J. B. Ward

CONTENTS

1

IN ORBIT FOR CHRIST

Best Use:

This program will especially appeal to young people and men.

Equipment Needed:

On a table in the front of the room place a large world globe, a lighted one if possible. At the base of the globe, place an open Bible, slightly elevated, so the open pages may be seen from the audience.

Use some type of a stand behind the table. From this stand hang spaceships on string or light wire. A stand such as women use for hanging freshly ironed clothes makes an excellent holder for the spaceships.

If the above is too much trouble or does not appeal, use a picture of the world. On butcher paper fastened together with tape for a large background, draw the world and spaceships with colored chalk, or paint with tempera paints.

If the place of the meeting is suitable, light-weight planes may be suspended from the light fixtures or the ceiling to give the whole room an atmosphere of air travel.

Scripture:

"I was not disobedient unto the heavenly vision" (Acts 26:19).

STORY:

In the year 1867, a boy baby was born in Dayton, Ohio. Four years later another baby boy came to bless the same family. The two boys were just like other boys in Dayton. They attended public school, had their share of boyhood fights, played in ball games. They were different, however, from the other boys in the dreams they had. They dreamed they would someday fly through the air. As they grew older, they began to work and invent engines and devices to make their dreams come true. Others began to laugh at the crazy Wright brothers, but Orville and Wilbur had no time to listen to laughter. They had a dream and they made their dream come true. In 1903, Orville was the first man to fly in a heavier-than-air machine. In their lifetime they were awarded many honors by scientific associations and schools.

Today we smile when we see a picture of one of the early planes. Flying has advanced. Space travel is the thing today, and we glibly talk of getting in orbit. A spaceship must be in orbit or it will not succeed in its purpose.

Just as the Wright brothers had to be the pioneers in air travel, so someone was the pioneer in starting————. [Name organization for which you are giving the devotional.]

Just as we have seen great and marvelous advancement in air travel so we want to see [our organization] go forward to greater heights under new leadership. All in the past have contributed to growth, but, standing on their shoulders, we expect our new officers to carry on in a great way.

CHARGE TO OFFICERS:

President

You are the one given the responsibility for the blast-off. The success of this launching will depend upon your vision and enthusiasm. You will have the responsibility for starting and stopping on time. The other officers will react to your leadership. You are not powerful enough in your own strength to blast off this satellite. There is a source of strength and power upon which you must call—the power of God. Call upon him before all major decisions. He who flung the world into space will help you to stay in orbit.

"Behold, he shall fly as an eagle" (Jer. 48:40).

Vice-president

To you falls the responsibility of standing ready to step in at a moment's notice and take the place of the president if something should go wrong. To you we give the responsibility of securing new recruits. Yours is not an easy task, but it is a rewarding one. You will find it easy to stay in orbit if you remember the Scripture: "Lo, I am with you alway, even unto the end of the world" (Matt. 28:20).

Secretary

As secretary you will be directly responsible for the countdown. You will need to be present at all the meetings. You must keep very accurate records of the proceedings. "Ye are our epistle written in our hearts, known and read of all men" (2 Cor. 3:2).

Treasurer

This organization cannot stay in orbit unless it has sufficient funds. Figures are always interesting if we remember they show the facts. No organization can be its best without some good person to keep the picture of their financial ability before them.

"For wisdom is a defence, and money is a defence: but the excellency of knowledge is, that wisdom giveth life to them that have it" (Eccl. 7:12).

Group Captains

You are the astronauts of this organization. You will explore space and bring back valuable information to those who wait. You will know why each member is absent and seek to bring them back. You will keep all members informed about the current happenings in the organization.

"Are they not all ministering spirits, sent forth to minister for them who shall be heirs of salvation?" (Heb. 1:14).

DEDICATION OF ALL OFFICERS:

So the launching pad is ready! All have been assigned their duties. Success depends upon each member of the group filling his place to the best of his ability and training.

We would ask the blessings of the one who created our world, one who gave us knowledge to conquer space, one who is over all and whom we seek to serve, upon our officers as we start a new year of service.

Close by having all to sing "Take My Life, and Let It Be."

2

HORN OF PLENTY

BEST USE:

For a group where there is an abundance of talent and leadership. This installation can be adapted to almost any age group.

EQUIPMENT NEEDED:

Secure a straw cornucopia and use it for a center-piece on a table at the front of the room. If fresh fruit is not available, use artificial fruit. As each officer is given a charge, he or she places an appropriate piece of fruit at the mouth of the cornucopia.

If you prefer, a flannel board may be used instead of the above. Place a cardboard horn of plenty on the flannel board. As each officer is called forward, give him cardboard or construction paper fruit to place on the board.

SCRIPTURE:

"He that tilleth his land shall have plenty of bread: but he that followeth after vain persons shall have poverty enough" (Prov. 28:19).

STORY:

During the Great Depression of the 1930's, many farm families found living hard. They were often discouraged.

The Billington family, living on a small farm in East Texas, were more discouraged than their neighbors. The father was in bed with a broken hip. The mother was a frail person. The farm work had to be shouldered by the two oldest boys, aged twelve and fourteen. There were three other children, all younger and all girls.

As Thanksgiving drew near, the children began to tell of the decorations the teacher was making at school.

They were especially impressed with the horn of plenty. The teacher had asked each child to bring something to place in the horn of plenty.

"What could we possibly take?" the little girls asked their mother.

"Food is so scarce I do not see how we can spare even a turnip," the mother told them.

The two boys did not want to see their sisters embarrassed or hurt at school. They began to think of a plan.

"Mother, if you will let all of us go to the creek bottom on Saturday, maybe we can gather some nuts," the boys suggested.

So, on Saturday, the five children went with buckets and sacks to the river bottom to hunt nuts. They searched diligently under the wild pecan trees, but others had been there before them, and they found only a few nuts.

Tired and weary they started toward home. As they came close to old Mrs. Thornton's house, they decided to stop and visit her a few moments.

"Would you children carry in some wood for me?" she asked. "My back has been hurting, and I have put off getting in wood."

Soon the children had the woodbox filled and told the old lady they must go home.

"If you would not mind carrying it, I will give you a big pumpkin," she told them.

"Oh, we would like to have a pumpkin. Mother can make a pie," the children told her.

"You know she can't make a pie without eggs," the smallest child said. "The eggs have to be sold to buy Daddy's medicine."

"That just reminded me," Mrs. Thornton smiled, "I need someone to gather my eggs. I think that old brown hen has a nest hidden someplace, and I haven't felt like hunting it."

The five children rushed out to the barn and chicken house and were soon rewarded by finding sixteen eggs.

"Now you just take half those eggs along with your pumpkin so your mother can make a pie."

The children were happy as they trudged along home. Maybe they would have a nice Thanksgiving.

"We still haven't anything to take to put in the horn of plenty," one of the girls lamented.

"Let's gather some red berries and yellow leaves. They will look pretty, even if they are not good to eat," the boys suggested.

So Monday found the children taking great armfuls of red berries and yellow leaves to school. Thanksgiving found the little family eating good pie garnished with a few nuts.

CHARGE TO OFFICERS:

There are times after promotion day when we feel our class needs leaders and workers. We, like the little children in the story, need to search for hidden talent. We must make the most of the talents we find if our horn of plenty is to be filled.

President

Come forward and place this bunch of grapes in the horn of plenty. Your duties will be like the grapes, a whole bunch! It is a high honor to be chosen president of this organization. You will face many decisions during the year. You will be able to make the right decisions by calling on God in prayer to help you.

Vice-president

Come forward and place this beautiful yellow lemon in the horn of plenty. You are a lovely person. I know you will not sound a sour note when you are called upon at the last minute to take charge of a meeting.

The president cannot function well without your help and support. As the president often calls upon you for some task, remember the words of Jesus: "Thou shalt love the Lord thy God with all thy heart, and with all thy soul, and with all thy mind. This is the first and great commandment. And the second is like unto it, Thou shalt love thy neighbour as thyself" (Matt. 22:37-39).

Secretary

Come forward and place this orange in the horn of plenty.

The orange is very pretty. It has a sweet odor. It is divided into neat sections. So you as secretary will keep your records neat and presentable. You will keep a sweet spirit, even when people question your accuracy.

Treasurer

Please place this peach in the horn of plenty. You will really be a peach if you keep account of the money coming in and going out of this organization.

Group Leaders

Group Leaders, each take an apple and place it in the horn of plenty.

Your "apples for the teacher" this year will be your close contact with your group. You will notify the teacher when she needs to know about illness or death.

CHARGE TO ALL OFFICERS:

"Then said Jesus unto his disciples, If any man will come after me, let him deny himself, and take up his cross, and follow me" (Matt. 16:24).

Remember the children in the story. What if they had told their elderly friend they had no time to help with her wood and eggs? They would have missed a blessing. What if they had not gone in search of something for the horn of plenty?

You as officers must search for those who need to be enlisted in your class.

DEDICATION:

If music is available to the old song, "Work, for the Night Is Coming" use it as a closing meditation. If not, read the words.

> Work, for the night is coming,
> Work thro' the morning hours;
> Work while the dew is sparkling,
> Work 'mid springing flowers;
> Work when the day grows brighter,
> Work in the glowing sun;
> Work, for the night is coming,
> When man's work is done.

3

THE MAGIC DIAL

From poster board or similar material, cut a large black telephone dial with holes for the numbers. If possible mount the dial on a white background. Use a screw or nail in the center so the dial can be turned around. Decorate with toy telephones. Have one phone book near the leader of the installation services. A few black wires or ribbons may be strung around for atmosphere.

Scripture:

"The Lord called Samuel again the third time. And he arose and went to Eli, and said, Here am I; for thou didst call me. And Eli perceived that the Lord had called the child" (1 Sam. 3:8).

Story:

Alexander Graham Bell was a boy with a problem. He loved his parents very much, but he was sad because his mother could not hear very well. Several others in his family had hearing problems. He would sit for hours and try to think of ways to help them hear. Early in life he began to try different ways to use sound. At the age of twenty-nine he patented the telephone. He could have said, "My loved ones have a problem but I can do nothing about it."

In place of giving up on his problem he studied sound. He studied voice physiology. He dreamed that there was some wonderful magic way to carry a person's voice. He found that magic way and helped millions of people to have an easier time. He helped our whole world to be a happier, better place because of his invention.

CHARGE TO OFFICERS:

Leader picks up the phone book and pretends to look up a name.

Teacher

[————], I see your name listed as teacher for this class. You're the magician who will need to dial the numbers of your class members many times. You must study hard to teach them the right answers to the questions and problems in their lives. You will find the answers to their needs in the Holy Bible. You will need to call the magic number of your Heavenly Father often and ask for his help and guidance.

President

[————], I see your name in the phone book and your new number for the year is president. You will make yourself heard each Sunday as you call the class to order and see that the right connections are ready for the service.

(*Leader looks in phone book*)

Vice-president

[—————], your name is listed as the vice-president. You have been chosen by your class to serve in this capacity because you always ring true when called upon in an emergency. You must promote the class in social and fellowship growth. You are to watch for ways to help your class grow.

"Blessed are those servants whom the lord when he cometh shall find watching" (Luke 12:37).

(*Leader looks in phone book*)

Secretary

[—————], the honor of being secretary has been bestowed upon you. You will record accurately and faithfully the progress of this class.

"Whatsoever ye do in word or deed, do all in the name of the Lord Jesus, giving thanks to God and the Father by him" (Col. 3:17).

Treasurer

[—————], your class shows a special kind of trust in you by electing you to handle the class funds. The magic dial will ring your number many times when there is need for money to be spent. Correct handling of class funds will be your responsibility.

"Let all things be done decently and in order" (1 Cor. 14:40).

(*Leader looking in phone book calls the names of all the group leaders.*)

Group Leaders

Ladies (or gentlemen), you are like some homes I know about; you will need several magic dials to keep up with all the members of your groups this year. Keep in touch and you will find not only blessings for yourself but will be a blessing to those you call.

"Behold, I have set before thee an open door" (Rev. 3:8).

DEDICATION:

After this installation service we hope each officer and leader in this class will think of the class each time you pass your phone. Keep a list of names or yearbook near the phone and determine to make this year count for Christ.

> Jesus is tenderly calling thee home,
> Calling today, calling today;
> Why from the sunshine of love wilt thou roam
> Farther and farther away?
>
> Calling today, . . . Calling today, . . .
> Jesus is calling,
> Is tenderly calling today.
>
> Jesus is calling the weary to rest
> Calling today, calling today;
> Bring him thy burden and thou shalt be blest;
> He will not turn thee away.
>
> Jesus is pleading; O list to His voice:
> Hear Him today, hear Him today;
> They who believe on His name shall rejoice;
> Quickly arise and away.

FANNY J. CROSBY

4

SEND THE LIGHT

BEST USE:

This theme can be used for a men's organization, a youth group, or women's mission group.

EQUIPMENT NEEDED:

The equipment for this installation may be very simple or very elaborate, according to the time and space available.

Use floor, table, and TV lights, one for each officer. (With these might be used a few old oil lamps or lanterns.)

If the group is small and space limited, use candles. On the center table use all sizes of candles, tall, short, thin, thick. As each officer is installed, hand him a small candle, lighted from the tallest one on the table.

SCRIPTURE:

"And God said, Let there be light: and there was light" (Gen. 1:3).

INTRODUCTORY STORY:

Two orphan boys left the city of Dallas around the year 1889 and sought work in West Texas. The oldest boy (we will call him Tim) vowed to his younger brother that he would take care of him and make him rich. The younger boy Randy was lonely in the vast open spaces and longed for the lights of the city of Dallas.

The boys found jobs on a ranch bordering New Mexico. Tim was very happy. He had a dream of owning a ranch someday. Randy tried to be happy because he had no one to depend upon except his brother. He longed to be back where there were people and excitement.

As soon as Tim became twenty-one he homesteaded a piece of land in New Mexico. The two boys lived in a dugout. A dugout is a house or room built by digging a hole in the ground and putting a top over it. The first year was very hard for Randy. Tim would go back to work for the rancher in order to make money for supplies. Randy would be left alone for several days at a time, staying in order to protect the claim on the land.

Randy wanted to run away, but that would not be easy when they were miles and miles from the nearest town. When it seemed he could not stand the loneliness and work any longer, Randy saw Tim coming home. His saddlebags were bulging, and there was a large flour sack tied on the back of the saddle.

Tim carefully untied the sack and took out a lamp. It was a kerosene lamp with a chimney.

"Now you can read at night," he told his brother.

"What?"

"I thought of that too," Tim smiled. "The rancher's wife sent you some of her books."

So the boys spent pleasant evenings reading by the new lamp. Randy never told Tim how near he came to running away. The two boys grew to be fine dependable men and Randy in later years became a minister. A light made the difference in their lives.

INSTALLATION:

(Leader turns on tallest light, or lights tallest candle.)

Always in our world the tallest light must represent Christ. The Light of our Christian world.

President

You *(call the president-elect by name)* will light the beautiful light. The president is expected to be beautiful in spirit at all times. You have been chosen for this office because you have proved yourself faithful at all times.

"The light shall shine upon thy ways" (Job 22:28).

Vice-president

One of the most noticeable things about a light is that it helps people see in darkness. Your light is bright because your place is not always an easy one to fill. You are to be dependable at all times. Yours is a light of loyalty. You will do your best to enlist new members and to make this organization grow.

"The Lord is my light and my salvation; whom shall I fear?" (Psalm 27:1).

Secretary

Yours is a light of service. One that is used often. You will light the way for good records. What is past and what is present will be at your finger tips at all times.

"Thy word is a lamp unto my feet, and a light unto my path" (Psalm 119:105).

Treasurer

For you we will turn on the light of faithfulness. Little children sometimes like to see a small light burning when they awake in the night. Your light will keep us from spending unwisely the funds available to our organization. Your records of our expenditures will be neat and accurate.

"For God, who commanded the light to shine out of darkness, hath shined in our hearts, to give the light of the knowledge of the glory of God in the face of Jesus Christ" (2 Cor. 4:6).

Program Chairman

For you we light a different light. Many people find this light very useful; it will burn soft, medium, or bright. It has a different shade from others. So your light must be one of variety. There must be variety, both in your programs and in the way they are presented.

"Christ shall give thee light" (Eph. 5:14).

All Other Officers

Your lights will be smaller and may be more alike, but your work is important. Jesus said, "Let your light so shine before men, that they may see your good works, and glorify your Father which is in heaven" (Matt. 5:16).

DEDICATION PRAYER:

Father take these officers, with their many lights and variety of talents, and use them in thy service.

Send the Light

There's a call comes ringing o'er the restless wave,
"Send the light!   Send the light!"
There are souls to rescue, there are souls to save,
Send the light!   Send the light!

We have heard the Macedonian call today,
"Send the light!   Send the light!"
And a golden off'ring at the cross we lay,
Send the light!   Send the light!

Let us pray that grace may ev'rywhere abound,
Send the light!   Send the light!
And a Christlike spirit ev'rywhere be found,
Send the light!   Send the light!

Let us not grow weary in the work of love,
Send the light!   Send the light!
Let us gather jewels for a crown above,
Send the light!   Send the light!

CHARLES H. GABRIEL

5

SHOES OF CHRISTIAN SERVICE

Best Use:

This is a program that can be adapted easily to almost any group of people, young or old. Shoes speak a language we all understand, for we all wear them.

Equipment Needed:

On a table at the front, place all types and kinds of shoes, both new and old, stylish and out-of-date. If it should be possible to buy miniature shoes at the variety store, get enough to hand a pair to each officer. If it is easier, cut out pictures of shoes, paste on cards and hand to each officer. If you should be having a banquet in connection with the program, decorate the tables with colored shoes cut out of construction paper.

If you happen to know a collector of ceramic shoes, you might borrow them for decorations.

Scripture:

"Then said the Lord to him, Put off thy shoes from thy feet: for the place where thou standest is holy ground" (Acts 7:33).

STORY:

Our two smallest granddaughters met at Christmastime. They were three years old and seemed quite happy to find they belonged to each other. As the happy excitement of taking gifts off the tree progressed, we noticed Sherri seemed to be pouting and brooding about something.

Sherri was wearing nice suede slippers. They were black and tied with a shoestring. In a moment she took off her slippers and went to her cousin. She took off Melonie's slippers which were a bright red with a brass buckle. Leaving the black ones with Melonie, Sherri went to a corner and began trying to get the red slippers on her chubby feet. They just would not fit. Sherri began to cry and only stopped when her mother promised that her next pair of slippers could be red ones.

As we listen to the installation service for our officers, some of you might be like little Sherri and feel the shoes of service assigned to you are not glamorous. Remember, though, we are all more comfortable in shoes that fit our feet. As we grow and progress, other opportunities for service come to us.

LEADER:

Look about you and see all the shoes gathered here at the front. We will pick the most worn and scuffed pair to represent the faithfulness and hard work of the officers in this organization this past year. They have served well, but their day of service is past. We are proud of the work they accomplished and the footprints they left for us to follow.

(Leader calls teacher to stand and face audience.)

Teacher

You have been elected by our church to teach this group. Your shoes are not new. You have taught faithfully many years. Your shoes show much signs of polishing and care. The psalmist of old wrote: "Thou hast set my feet in a large room" (Psalm 31:8). Indeed your feet are set in a large room of service for the coming year, may God bless and keep you as you seek to help these class members grow in grace and knowledge.

(Leader calls president to stand and face group.)

President

I have selected a pair of stout walking shoes for you. You will have to walk ahead of the others in order to lead them in activities and projects. These shoes may take you into difficult places as you seek to win new members or to bring back one who has drifted away. I hope by the end of your term of service these shoes show many signs of service well rendered.

"He will keep the feet of his saints, and the wicked shall be silent in darkness; for by strength shall no man prevail" (1 Sam. 2:9).

(Leader calls vice-president to stand and face group.)

Vice-president

I selected a nice serviceable pair of house slippers for you. Just when you think you are set to rest awhile, your teacher or president will call upon you to take charge of the meeting. You will be busy planning social events for the class, so, besides your house shoes, you will need this pair of high-heeled party slippers. You must be versatile and uncomplaining when it is time to change.

"How beautiful are thy feet with shoes, O prince's daughter!" (Song of Sol. 7:1).

(Leader calls secretary to stand and face group.)

Secretary

We have such a neat dainty pair or shoes for you. They symbolize how neat and dainty your records will be kept. You will report regularly on the activities of the class. You will see that each person has literature at the proper time.

People usually take better care of fragile, dainty things, so we know you will take your records seriously and care for them tenderly.

"Every wise woman buildeth her house: but the foolish plucketh it down with her hands" (Prov. 14:1).

(Leader calls group leaders to stand and face group.)

Group Leaders

The Indians have a saying, "Judge no man until you have worn his moccasins for a week."

Often you will grow impatient with those on your groups who make excuses week after week and fail to attend. Just keep trying to win them. Remember you have not worn their shoes a week.

For you group leaders I selected a shoe with a soft rubber sole. These shoes will wear well, yet they feel soft as you walk. You must be persistent, you must wear well and you will see your group grow spiritually.

DEDICATION PLEDGE:

As all of you put on your shoes of Christian service I would like for you to read with me the pledge I have handed you.

> I pledge my loyalty to my class and church.
> I pledge and promise to be true to the trust
>   which the church has placed in me.
> I promise to fulfil my duty as a worker to
>   the best of my ability—
>   to study, plan, pray, and work for the
>   best interest of the class.
> With God's help I will be the best worker that I can.

6

KEYS FOR UNLOCKING DOORS
OF SERVICE

BEST USE:

For women's or men's groups. Could be used in a small church for installing all the officers of the church at a banquet.

EQUIPMENT NEEDED:

This can be very simple with a large red heart made of cardboard on which construction paper keys can be hung as each officer comes forward. Or, for a church group, make a very large ring of cardboard, and cover it with gold Christmas foil. Place thumbtacks all around the ring to hold the keys of the different groups as they come forward to be installed. Have enough keys cut out of construction paper for each person. On the key type an appropriate Scripture passage. If this is a church project, be sure to use as many of the people as possible. Have a decorations committee, a food committee, a program committee. Select a good master of ceremonies to introduce the installing officer.

STORY:

Mary and John were called suddenly to the bedside of John's mother. They had to travel three hundred miles to get there. Hurriedly, they packed a few clothes and started late in the afternoon.

About halfway to their destination, they became so tired and sleepy they decided to stop at a restaurant. Each automatically locked the door of the car.

When they came out to resume their journey, John felt in all his pockets and could not find the key to the car. Mary searched her purse for her key, but she had changed purses and left the key at home.

"We were careless and locked the key inside," John mourned.

"I have often thought we should have an extra key made and placed with a magnet under the hood," Mary said.

After trying to open a window with a wire, they gave up and broke the window with a rock.

They had wasted much precious time, had to be out the expense of a new window, and were cold as they drove on through the night, all because they were careless.

The new officers to be installed tonight will find they must guard well their key of new service, keep it available at all times, and use it often to unlock new avenues of service.

You, too, are starting on an urgent mission to last three hundred and sixty-five days. If you neglect your key and fail to keep your door of service open, much precious time will be wasted. You will be an expense to your church and a disappointment to those who look to you for leadership.

Before we start I would like to read a poem and dedicate it to those who have served so faithfully during this past year.

> I have hoped, I have planned and striven;
> To the will I have added the deed;
> The best that was in me I've given;

I have prayed but the gods would not heed.
I have dared when faced with disaster;
I have battled and broken my lance;
I am bruised by that pitiless master
The weak and the timid call Chance.
I am old, I am bent, I am cheated
Of all I had hoped to win;
But nay, I am not defeated,
For today again I begin.

(AUTHOR UNKNOWN)

Will the pastor please come to the front? For you, we have a golden key to new evaluations. This is a larger key than the others. As you have the vision of what our church can accomplish, so you will lead us to greater heights of service this new year. Your key will open a larger door of service than any other. You will find the way to turn this key in the lock as you read and pray for each new officer.

Will all the Sunday School department superintendents please come to the front to receive your keys? For you, we have purple keys representing royal leadership. You must turn the key in the lock on the door of enthusiasm. As you inspire your teachers to work, so will your department grow. For you, I will hang a key smaller than the pastor's, but larger than the others upon this heart key ring.

Will all the teachers in the church come to the front and receive your keys? For you, we have keys colored blue. Blue keys will turn the lock in the door of loyalty and faith. As you are faithful and loyal to your trust, this Sunday School will grow.

Will all the secretaries come forward? For you, we have white keys. These represent the clean white pages you have to fill with records and minutes in the future.

Will the church treasurer and all the class treasurers come to stand near this ring of keys?

For each of you, I have a yellow key representing gold. This key turns the lock on our material investments in this organization. We hope each member will be a true steward and each of you will be accurate with your accounts.

All the pianists and song leaders for the church and departments please come to the front. For you, we will hang on the ring a green key. Green represents growth. As we enjoy your leadership in music, we will be inspired to attend and our services will grow.

Will all the group captains stand and come to the front? For you, we saved the color red. Your key will unlock the door of sacrifice. It will take sacrificial service for others if you are to keep in touch and minister to your groups.

Mr. —————, will you come forward and accept a key for other types of offices we have not called? Will all who hold some office we have not mentioned please stand where you are?

For all of you we hang a brown key on the key ring. Brown is a color never outstanding, yet always serviceable. What would we do without all the people who fit in some place and quietly go about serving and making the work go?

All of you stand and join hands with each other as we sing a verse of the song, "Onward Christian Soldiers." At the close of the song as you silently pray our pastor will lead in a prayer of dedication.

For a New Period of Service

May you have enough happiness to keep you sweet;
Enough trials to keep you strong;
Enough sorrow to keep you human;
Enough hope to make your heart sing;
Enough labor to keep you from rust;
Enough leisure to make you broad;
Enough religion to make you value the best;
Enough of love of Christ in your soul to make you glad to serve.

(AUTHOR UNKNOWN)

7

MEXICAN GRAB BAG

BEST USE:

For a group of young people or a children's mission organization such as Girls' Auxiliary or Royal Ambassadors.

EQUIPMENT NEEDED:

A piñata (pronounced pin-yah-tah) can be purchased at a gift shop or from one specializing in party materials. Get one filled with candy. At the close, this can be broken by the whole group and the candy used as refreshments. If a more elaborate meal is preferred, be sure to serve some type of Mexican food.

If some of the young people have Mexican clothes, encourage them to wear them. For atmosphere, have someone play some numbers on a guitar.

The sky is the limit on decorations. Borrow all kinds of Mexican vases, rugs, and silver jewelry. Display these.

Put a large paper bag on a table. The bag can be decorated with colorful Mexican scenes taken from a child's coloring book and pasted on the bag.

On one end of a string, tie the name of each officer to be installed. On the other end, tie an appropriate toy which is kept out of sight in the bag until the officer pulls the string with his name on it.

Suggested miniature toys to hang on the strings and be pulled from the grab bag are: for the president, a small wooden or rubber gavel or hammer; for the vice-president, a teapot; for the program chairman, a book or a Bible portion; for the secretary, a small notebook and a pencil (use bright colors); for the treasurer, a bank; for the musicians, a small piano and a baton (if these cannot be purchased, make some music notes out of cardboard and cover them with gold foil); for the publicity chairman or reporter, a toy telephone; for group leaders, small cars.

If the group is small and expenses have to be considered, all the above may be cut out of toy catalogs and pasted on cards.

SCRIPTURE:

"Seek ye the Lord while he may be found, call ye upon him while he is near" (Isa. 55:6).

STORY:

Myra was a Mexican woman who had been very happy. For many years her husband worked for a West Texas farmer, and her lot was easier than most of her friends. Her son grew up to be a fine young man and finished high school. Then one day a tragedy came; the husband was killed in a tractor accident. Myra moved into the nearest town and started working as a nursery keeper for a church. Myra's son went into military service, but he was able to send his mother only a small allotment each month. Life was now hard for the Mexican woman. Some years before losing her husband she had trusted Christ and joined a Baptist church.

Her strong belief in God helped her keep working and trying. The mothers who brought their children to the nursery learned to trust and appreciate her.

After a few years, a letter came from her son asking her to make a trip to his army base. He was to receive an honor, and he wanted his mother present.

Myra wanted to go more than anything in the world, but, when she checked the price of a round-trip bus ticket, it was close to one hundred dollars. The money she would have to spend on lodging and food would make the trip more than she could possibly afford.

Myra began to pray and ask God to show her the way to make the trip. She ate almost nothing all week. Rent still had to be paid and bills met. She could not in any way raise one hundred dollars. Still she prayed. In all likelihood her boy would be sent overseas soon. She wanted very much to go.

The pastor's wife asked Myra to keep her children one day while she made a trip to a meeting. Myra always kept the children free because she felt it was something she could do to help the pastor and his wife.

This time she went to the pastor's home with a heavy heart. She could have picked cotton that day and made a little money.

After school, the children wanted Myra to walk with them to the grocery store. At the store, a big dairy company was giving away small samples of a new kind of cottage cheese. Each person signed his name and address and took the sample. Myra and the children all signed the slips and took the cottage cheese home to eat.

When Myra reached home, there was a letter in her box from her son's commanding officer. The letter especially invited her to be at the camp the next week to see her son decorated for his outstanding work.

Myra sat down and cried as she prayed: "God please work one of your miracles and let me find a way to go."

As Myra sat there praying, there was a knock on the door. She opened the door, and there stood the man who had been giving away the cottage cheese.

"We were going to give a $100 prize to the name we drew at the close of the day," he smiled. "Your name is the one to win."

"God worked a miracle!" Myra began to laugh as she cried.

"You mean cottage cheese worked a miracle," the man told her.

Then Myra told him about her son and the letter asking her to make a trip.

Reporters came and took Myra's picture and wrote the story about how God and cottage cheese worked a miracle.

God uses many things to carry on his work. In this organization he has chosen to use this new group of officers to work his miracles this coming year. Won't it be exciting as you fill your place to see wonderful things happening?

CHARGE TO OFFICERS:

President

You are given the privilege of pulling the first string from this grab bag. (*President pulls string marked "President."*) So you have a small gavel. You will be expected to keep order at the meetings. You will start and close meetings. When your gavel is silent between meetings, you will still ponder and think on ways to make the organization grow.

You will promote plans for helping each member enjoy his work better.

Vice-president

You may pull the second string. (*Pull out a toy teapot.*) Oh, a teapot. That must mean you are to promote social activity in the group. People enjoy programs and get-togethers. You will seek to plan and encourage these meetings. When the president is absent you will preside in his place.

Secretary

Please let us see what you can draw from the grab bag. A notebook and pencil! How exciting! You will be writing all through the year. We may forget things that happen but your records will always give us the facts.

Treasurer

This looks like a very strong string. Please don't keep us in suspense. Pull it out of the bag and let us see. (*Treasurer pulls out a small bank.*) We will face the year with the utmost tranquility with your taking care of our bank.

Pianist and Chorister

No meeting is quite so beautiful and meaningful as the one where there is good music. Please pull your strings and let us see what the grab bag has for you (*a toy piano and a music baton*). What fun! Please place this piano and baton where you will be sure to see them each meeting day and remember we need you to be present.

Publicity Chairman

You might be called just a plain reporter in some organizations. We expect you not only to report about our meetings but to publicize them with posters and word of mouth, so you will find a megaphone at the end of your string.

Group Leaders

Ask the group leaders to come to the front and pull all the remaining strings but one. (*They all draw out toy cars.*)

These cars represent a way you could contact your group from time to time. A personal visit always helps. You will make new friends as you travel about, and you will learn to love old friends better as you know them better.

DEDICATION:

(*Leader draws out the last string. Attached is a legal looking envelope containing a contract, which he reads aloud.*) "We pledge to serve to the best of our ability this coming year. We will not willingly neglect the meetings. We will study our duties and strive to carry them out."

Will all of you say, "I will" to this contract?

Read the following:

> You are the fellow that has to decide
> Whether you'll do it or toss it aside.
> You are the fellow who makes up his mind
> Whether you'll lead or linger behind.

(AUTHOR UNKNOWN)

PRAYER:

Our Father, bless each officer here today. Give them joy in the task they have just begun. Bless their efforts great and small. We pray in the name of Christ.

8

SHIPS GO SAILING

BEST USE:

For any type of mission or civic organization. The types of officers mentioned can be adapted to other similar types.

EQUIPMENT NEEDED:

Cover a table with water-blue paper. On one end place a construction paper lighthouse. Stand this lighthouse on a base of small rocks. If possible, place a small light inside the lighthouse. On the other end of the table place a model ship, or toy ship. In the center, elevated at the back of the table, place an open Bible with a sign reading, "Our Compass for 19—." If you wish to be more elaborate, use a picture of Christ with a paper anchor attached to a small piece of rope at the base.

Cut small ships out of construction paper and hand to each officer as he is installed. Toy boats can be used.

SCRIPTURE:

"They that go down to the sea in ships, that do business in great waters; these see the works of the Lord, and his wonders in the deep" (Psalm 107:23-24).

STORY:

Tom grew up in a fine Christian home. His parents shielded him from all evil and ugliness. They took him to the best places, and he knew all the best people.

People were shocked when Tom left home at twenty-one and joined the Navy.

"Why did Tom go away from home and join the Navy?" they asked.

Tom's parents were disappointed and heartbroken. They had been very careful to give him much.

When the maid went into Tom's room to clean it and prepare it for a time when he might come home, she stopped and looked for a minute at a picture on the wall.

The picture was very beautiful. It was of a ship under full sail on a calm and peaceful sea.

"How long has this picture been in Tom's room?" she asked his mother.

"Since he was a very small boy," the mother replied. "He loved to look at the ship."

"Perhaps it was ever before him, a dream that he too would someday sail on the ocean," the wise maid said.

We are about to go sailing into a new year of service. We, too, must keep ever before us the goal of our organization.

> Forget each kindness that you do
> As soon as you have done it,
> Forget the praise that falls to you
> The moment you have won it,
> Forget the slanders that you hear
> Before you can repeat it,

Forget each slight, each spite, each sneer,
  Wherever you may meet it.

Remember every kindness done
  To you what e'er its measure,
Remember praise by others won
  And pass it on with pleasure,
Remember every promise made
  And keep it to the letter,
Remember those who lend you aid,
  And be a grateful debtor.

Remember all the happiness
  That comes your way in living;
Forget each worry and distress,
  Be hopeful and forgiving,
Remember good, remember truth
  Remember heaven's above you
And you will find through age and youth
  True joys and hearts to love you.

(AUTHOR UNKNOWN)

CHARGE TO OFFICERS:

Will all the officers come to the front and sit in this semi-circle of chairs?

Now we are ready to set sail to do business in great waters.

Before we launch out on our voyage we must have equipment, but first we need a pilot. Christ gave himself for us. What better pilot could we have! There must be complete trust in him. He is to have complete control over our lives as we sail this sea of service in 19—.

(If possible pause here and have a soloist sing a verse of "Who Will Our Pilot Be?")

> We sail along toward the harbor light
> Over the great life sea;
> The breakers roar and the waves dash high,
>   Who will our pilot be?
>
> The Christ will our Pilot be, . . .
> A wonderful Guide is he; . . .
> So we'll sail, sail, sail,
> Christ will our Pilot be.

LIZZIE DeARMOND

Two things we desperately need on a ship, a compass and an anchor. The compass will give us directions when we feel hopelessly lost and afraid. What better compass than God's Holy Word?

(Same soloist sing a verse of "I Know the Bible Is True.")

> I know the Bible was sent from God,
> The Old, as well as the New;
> Inspired and holy, the living Word,
> I know the Bible is true.

B. B. McKINNEY

When it seems that dissension and trouble beset our ship of service, we must cast our anchor to one who can hold our ship steady in a storm. Our anchor must be our love for Christ.

Along the way we will see a lighthouse. This lighthouse is our church. It reminds us to keep a safe distance from the rocky shores of things and places not approved by our parent organization.

President

We will see these different officers flying flags from our ship as we sail. To you, Mr. President, will go the responsibility of flying the flag of "LEADERSHIP." You will seek to lead in an executive capacity.

Vice-president

You will be flying the flag of "MEMBERSHIP," ever seek to enlist new members. Always be ready to lend a helping hand to the president.

Social Chairman

To you comes the responsibility of flying the flag of "FELLOWSHIP." Don't mind shaking hands with the members. Plan social events for them. Fly this flag from the very highest point on the ship of service.

Secretary

Keep your flag in a book for it is the flag of "PENMANSHIP." You must have accuracy and patience as you keep the records complete.

Other Officers

(Some ships you may fit to the other offices are: "sponsorship," "stewardship," "partnership," "friendship," "seamanship," "craftsmanship." Use appropriate remarks.)

CLOSING:

This can be an exciting year if we sail our ship of service into the "Port of Good Deeds."

It is better with him when the billows dash high,
   On the breast of the mad Galilee;
Though the Master may sleep he will wake at our cry,
Or he'll come on the waves saying: "Peace, it is I."
Better this than a calm when he is not nigh,
   Or without him to sail a smooth sea.

(AUTHOR UNKNOWN)

PRAYER OF DEDICATION:

We know not what storms and waves await us tomorrow, but we dedicate ourselves to thee today. May we each determine to make this voyage a successful one. Give us joy in cooperation and working together. We ask in the name of Christ our Master Pilot.

9

TRIP INTO THE FUTURE

Best Use:

For teachers and officers in a department of the Sunday School, or for a group of teachers and officers working with pre-teens or younger.

Equipment Needed:

Take several large sheets of cardboard or poster board and paste all kinds of colorful pictures of trains, planes, cars (and, if possible to find, some horses and donkeys) on the posters. Arrange these at the front on easels. For effect you could arrange several overnight kits, suitcases, and brief-cases as a display. If a travel agency is located in your city, you may get all kinds of folders and may even borrow some posters to use. Remember your theme is "A Trip into the Future," so anything pertaining to travel may be used.

Scripture:

"I will go in the strength of the Lord God: I will make mention of thy righteousness, even of thine only" (Psalm 71:16).

STORY:

One summer we were planning a long trip into the far Eastern states. We had only two weeks to make the trip of about four thousand miles, there and back. How we did plan and prepare! We knew just how many miles each day we must travel to keep on schedule. We knew how much money our budget would allow us to spend each day. We notified our relatives when we would call home to let them know how we were progressing.

Then the day came and we were actually in the car and on our way!

CHARGE TO OFFICERS:

Some of you officers and teachers have known for some time you were going to take this trip into the future with a group of pupils; you have had study courses and talked to your pastor. I hope you have at least started visiting your pupils, but tonight you officially start on this trip into the future as a worker in this department.

> No service in itself is small;
>   None great though earth it fill:
> But that is small that seeks its own,
>   And great that seeks God's will.
>
> Then hold my hand, most gracious God,
>   Guide all my goings still;
> And let it be my life's one aim,
>   To know and do Thy will.
>
> (AUTHOR UNKNOWN)

Will all the department superintendents come to the front and stand ready to board the plane for our trip into the future?

Superintendents

You have often heard it said, "As go the parents, so go the children."

As you are enthusiastic and energetic, so will your teachers be.

I will give each of you a fast jet plane, for you must go fast and lead the way for the department you serve. You will spend time on advanced planning and emphases for this group. I hope that even now you have goals set for your department and plans for the twelve months to follow.

Teachers

As the department superintendents are being seated, will the teachers please come to the front?

As teachers, you must have good road maps for a year of travel. (If possible write your state highway department ahead of time and secure enough road maps for each teacher.)

Remember, you do not travel alone. A group of pupils looks to you to lead the way.

Years ago, in Scotland, an aging minister had only one convert during the year. The leaders in the church came to the minister and said, "All this year you have won only one person, and that a young boy. We believe your usefulness is over."

The minister, after offering his resignation, sat alone as the people left the church. Tears of sadness filled his eyes. He was old and worn out. The boy, who was the lone convert for the year, came back into the church and walked to the side of his pastor.

"Pastor, do you think if I work hard in school I can someday be a minister and lead people as you have?"

Years later the "just a young boy" won by the old minister was honored by nobles and princes. He was a great leader and a translator of the Bible. His work was great as he opened the way for worldwide missionary causes. He was Robert Moffat.

I charge you, as teachers, to teach each Sunday as if every pupil would become a Robert Moffat. You will live out your day of usefulness, but those you teach will pick up the torch and carry on.

Study your pupils, their homes and problems. Teach to meet those needs. Use well your guide map, for you will not have this same opportunity again.

Pianist and Chorister

Some mornings you will be tempted to miss your train. You will think, *I am only used a few moments and it is easier to miss today.*

Music is important to all of God's children. It encourages us when we are sad. It releases our joy when we are happy.

(*Give to each a toy instrument of some kind.*)

You must travel into the future along a path of self-renunciation and self-sacrifice.

"I will sing unto the Lord, because he hath dealt bountifully with me" (Psalm 13:6).

SECRETARY:

I am sure you feel at times you are riding on a slow donkey while the others in the department flash by on jets.

Records are tedious and slow, but think how important they are.

The teacher might be busy and fail to notice some child's being absent. You need to hand each teacher a list of her absent pupils each Sunday.

(Give each secretary a toy donkey or a toy Model T or any type of slower transportation available.)

DEDICATION OF ALL OFFICERS:

Let each officer cherish the vision of the future. "But this I say, brethren, the time is short" (1 Cor. 7:29).

> A Builder builded a temple
> He wrought it with grace and skill;
> Pillars and groins and arches,
> All fashioned to work his will.
> "It shall never decay;
> Great is thy skill, O builder!
> Thy fame shall endure for aye."
>
> A Teacher builded a temple
> With loving and infinite care,
> Planning each arch with patience,
> Laying each stone with prayer.
> None praised her unceasing efforts
> None knew of her wondrous plan,
> For the temple the teacher builded
> Was unseen by the eyes of man.
>
> Gone is the Builder's temple,
> Crumbled into the dust;
> Low lies each stately pillar,
> Food for consuming rust.
> But the temple the Teacher builded

Will last while the ages roll,
For that beautiful unseen temple
Was a child's immortal soul.

(AUTHOR UNKNOWN)

PRAYER:

Father, as we enter into the future, may we each plan to be faithful to Christ and to our trust as leaders of this department. Fill us with zeal for the trip and may we be alert to the multiplied opportunities which we will encounter along the way. In the name of the one who traveled before us, our Lord Jesus Christ, we pray. Amen.

10

CHAINS OF SERVICE

BEST USE:

For a class or club meeting in a home or small room. This is planned for all present, officers and members, to participate.

EQUIPMENT NEEDED:

Secure a package of light-weight construction paper in a pretty gold shade. Cut all the paper in one-and-one-half-inch strips across the short way of the paper. Prepare as many strips as the number of people you anticipate will attend. Take the rest of the paper strips and glue them together in a long paper chain. Use this for your decoration.

You can hang the chain from a light fixture, or arrange it as a center of interest near the speaker. The speaker will need to be near a card table or small table of some kind.

On the table by the leader, place a bottle of glue and the extra strips of gold paper. As each officer is called, ask him to catch hold of the chain and glue on a link for himself. As they stand holding the end of the chain, each new officer called will glue on a link and stand next in line. It may be necessary for the leader to have some short lengths of chain on the table to fasten on in order to reach from one officer to the other. When the service is completed, everyone in the room should be standing holding the chain, and it should make a complete circle of the ones present.

SCRIPTURE:

"I have compared thee, O my love, to a company of horses in Pharaoh's chariots. Thy cheeks are comely with rows of jewels, thy neck with chains of gold" (Song of Sol. 1:9-10).

STORY:

A few years ago there were five children living in the slums of a city. Often they were hungry and cold. Their father was a drunkard, and the mother was often unable to find work.

As the children prowled about the city looking in trash cans and garbage heaps, they discovered a man who was in the business of buying scrap iron and other types of junk.

"You children need money and I will pay you by the pound for all the pieces of iron you bring me," the man told them.

Now the little fellows had a goal in life. The boys would scatter out and search for little bits of iron to sell. They made a few nickels and dimes, often the difference between being fed or being hungry.

One day the least child found a long heavy iron chain. The chain was too heavy for him to budge it from its hiding place. He pulled and pulled, but he was just too light to move it.

The little boy sat down and hugged the end of the great heavy chain in his arms. Tears of frustration fell from his eyes. He was tired and exhausted, but he kept sitting and holding the chain for fear someone else might find it if he went away. Slowly his eyes closed, and he went to sleep.

A lady coming out to bring her garbage, saw the child,

but she only shrugged her shoulders and went back to her own uncomfortable apartment.

When the children gathered home, they missed little Tim.

"You must go look for him," the mother urged. "He must be lost."

The father coming in, for once sober, asked what was wrong.

"Please come with us to hunt him," the children urged. "It is getting so dark."

So the father and children started to look for Tim. The children knew where they had parted to search for scrap iron so they went there and started to look.

As they went down the alleys, one of the boys began calling, "Tim, Tim, where are you?"

Tim heard their voices and woke up. "Here I am, come and get me."

When the boys and father found Tim, he would not turn loose of the chain.

"Tim, we will all help you carry it and it will not be too heavy," the brother said.

"Why do you want the chain?" the father asked.

"To sell and buy food."

"My boys have to sell junk to get food!"

"Yes, we do. You spend your money on whiskey."

The man grabbed one end of the chain, the boys each lifted links and so they all went home carrying the heavy old log chain.

The story had a happy ending, for the father was ashamed he had been so neglectful of his family and promised to change his ways.

The children found they could do better working together than separately.

CHARGE TO OFFICERS:

President ————————, will you please come forward? You are about to take up the chain of duty. This golden chain will bind you to the responsibility of leading this organization. You will be chained to this group with love for our Lord and for the members who look to you for leadership.

Vice-president ————————, you, too, will bind yourself with the golden chains of service. You will ever be gracious. Your kindness and interest in this organization will shine as bright as the gold chain you are holding. You have been chosen carefully for this position. We are confident you will not break the chain of service.

Secretary ————————, your hands will be very busy recording the events taking place at the meetings. Your part of this golden chain will be kept neatly and accurately. Like the little boys in the story, you will find working together much more rewarding than working alone.

"Whatsoever thy hand findeth to do, do it with thy might" (Eccl. 9:10).

Treasurer ————————, your chain may not be too heavy with money, but it is very important that we know what we spend our funds for and have a record kept of the expenditure. You will see that the portion of this chain of service which falls to you is kept ready for inspection at all times.

Group leaders (*call names as they stand, and give each some chain to fasten on the long one*), ————————, ————————, ————————, the chain of service grows longer and longer as we see you ready to carry your share. You must be cooperative with the other officers and help them keep up-to-date on the state of affairs in the organization.

Now I have asked —————— to give some chain to each member present and to help them fasten their chain to the chain of the officers. As we stand in this circle, we are all holding the chain of service. We each have a responsibility to carry our part of the chain. We should ever strive to be present, to help with the programs, and to work together as brothers or sisters in the Lord.

Dedication Poem

If none but you in the world so wide
Had found the Christ for his daily guide
Would the things you do and the things you say
Lead others to live in His blessed way?

Ah, friends of the Christ, in the world today
Are many who watch you upon your way,
And look to the things you say and do
To measure the Christian standard true!

Then guard this treasure that you possess,
This power to hurt, or help, or bless;
And live so close to the standard true
That others may safely follow you!

(AUTHOR UNKNOWN)

PRAYER:

As we stand bound together with this chain of golden paper, may we in our hearts feel a chain of God's golden love binding us to our duty of service. Give to each person in the circle a happy useful year. Amen.

11

SEARCH FOR GOLD

BEST USE:

Use for installing officers of a club or class.

EQUIPMENT NEEDED:

If you want a simple installation for a small group, use the following equipment. Cut large circles from gold Christmas paper or construction paper. On the back of each circle write a Scripture passage given below. Hand one to the officer being installed as you talk to them.

If you want to use this for a more significant group, buy a can of gold spray paint and spray a group of articles, such as different shaped bottles and cans or boxes. Use these as an interest center. Place them on a table covered with gold crepe paper. You might place among the gold bottles and cans a few objects covered with brown crepe paper to look like rocks. Put a flat cake pan on the front of the table (for panning for gold), and in the cake pan put the circles of yellow paper with the Scriptures on them to be given each officer.

SCRIPTURE:

President: "That the trial of your faith, being much more precious than of gold that perisheth, though it be tried with fire, might be found unto praise and honour and glory at the appearing of Jesus Christ" (1 Peter 1:7).

Vice-president: "The law of thy mouth is better unto me than thousands of gold and silver" (Psalm 119:72).

Secretary: "If thou return to the Almighty . . . then shalt thou lay up gold as dust, and the gold of Ophir as the stones of the brooks" (Job 22:23-24).

Group Leaders: "He brought them forth also with silver and gold: and there was not one feeble person among their tribes" (Psalm 105:37).

Teacher: "Receive my instruction, and not silver; and knowledge rather than choice gold" (Prov. 8:10).

STORY:

Two young men left their homes in the East to travel to California in search of gold. The year was 1849, and word had trickled back to their home of fabulous riches to be had for the taking.

They left eager and willing to work. Both promised loved ones they would return vastly wealthy.

In California, they bought equipment and started to search for gold. They separated over a small disagreement, and went in different directions.

They both struggled on for many weeks in their quest for gold. Ever they were seeking, but they were often disappointed.

At last Tom found enough to fill his pockets. He returned to the city. There he thought of the home in the East and decided he preferred seeking the gold of happiness and contentment at home. He returned home, married, and became a success as far as his town was concerned.

The other boy, Will, determined to make himself a very

wealthy man. On his trips to town he would take all the gold he had found and buy pieces of property with it. Then he would go back to the search again. Years passed. Will owned more and more lots and houses in the city, but he had no real joy in his success. One day he asked himself why he did not quit the constant search and go home to show what a great man he had become.

Putting his business in order, he started back to the East. When he reached his hometown, he hurried to his parents' home, but a stranger opened the door. "Where are my parents?"

"They died several months ago. The house had to go to pay for their funerals."

The wealthy gold miner walked the streets and looked for a friendly face. At last he came to a small store run by his old friend Tom.

"Tom, I am very wealthy. I stayed until I reached my goal," he bragged.

"That is fine, Will. I decided my goal was for happiness and contentment." Tom pointed to a small boy playing on the floor in the corner. "There is something worth more than all the gold you found."

Will returned to the West, but often during the lonely years of old age he asked himself, "Did I search for the wrong gold?"

CHARGE TO OFFICERS:

Like the boys in the story, as officers you will be searching for gold to make your organization better this coming year.

There are many places in the world where people have staked out claims to search for gold or precious metals.

Only a few of the claims staked out are being worked today.

The things this organization can accomplish this year are like the gold claims. They can be accomplished, or they can be neglected and forgotten.

President ————————, you have been chosen as president of the ———————— class for the coming year. As we realize that gold is a precious metal, may you realize how precious are the ones you have been selected to lead this year. May you find gold in prayer and service as you stand before the group sparkling as gold sparkles in the sunlight.

Vice-president ————————, you will find from history that the process of obtaining gold is an intricate and tiring one. By constant work, you will be able to enlist new members. As it comes your turn to preside, you will seek to point others in the direction in which they, too, may seek gold and find it by taking part in the activities of the group.

Secretary ————————, you will keep a golden record of this group. Your reports will be so accurate and clear it will be as if they were written on leaves of gold.

Treasurer ————————, you will recall that gold is a symbol of material wealth. While this organization is concerned chiefly with spiritual wealth, you will still keep a record of the way we show that spiritual wealth by our gifts and the way we spend the money.

Group Leaders (*call names of all group leaders and have them stand*), ————————, ————————, gold is produced in many countries: Africa, United States, Brazil, Russia, and Mexico. So are your groups made up of a variety of people. Some will be easy to contact and lead while others may seem hard to reach and be lacking in a spirit of cooperation. You are to search for the gold in the lives of the ones assigned to you. I feel sure you will receive a blessing as you seek to win each for better service.

Teacher —————, as gold is polished and shines for all to see the beauty of its radiance, so you as teacher have a shining opportunity to teach and to win for Christ. Consider each member of your class as a nugget of gold to be carefully guarded and watched over.

To all members present: to all of you I would hold up a golden standard, the standard of doing your best.

READ THIS POEM:

> My Father is rich in houses and lands,
> He holdeth the wealth of the world in his hands!
> Of rubies and diamonds, of silver and gold,
> His coffers are full, he has riches untold.
>
> I'm a child of the King,
> A child of the King:
> With Jesus my Saviour,
> I'm a child of the King.

HARRIET E. BUELL

PRAYER OF DEDICATION:

Dear Father, look into our hearts today. They are unpolished, unrefined, and as rough nuggets. Help each of us to determine to seek to live up to the gold standard we have had set before us today. Help us to search for gold in the lives of those with whom we serve, in the name of Christ.

12

GALAXY OF STARS

Best Use:

Can be used in a small church for the installation of all church officers at one supper meeting.

Can be used in a simple form for a small group, class or club.

Equipment Needed:

If possible, secure a Christmas star that can be placed in a prominent place and lighted.

Under the lighted star, place a table with an open Bible, elevated so as to show from all parts of the room.

For each person to be installed, make a star about five inches across and cover with foil. Get one good pattern and make all the stars by the same pattern.

Scripture:

"They that be wise shall shine as the brightness of the firmament; and they that turn many to righteousness as the stars for ever and ever" (Dan. 12:3).

"There is one glory of the sun, and another glory of the moon, and another glory of the stars: for one star differeth from another star in glory" (1 Cor. 15:41).

(*Parts of these Scriptures may be quoted as different officers are installed.*)

STORY:

It is estimated that there are between two and three thousand millions of stars in the sky. There is no sight more beautiful than a starry sky on a summer night. One feels relaxed and near to God just sitting and looking at the heavens. The stars in heaven are God's creation, and they are perfect for his purpose.

Tonight we are going to think for a moment about the morning star. In Revelation 2:28 we read, "I will give him the morning star."

In our modern day when the word "star" is mentioned we think first about someone outstanding in the world of show business. We are about to place in the position of stars in our church people elected for service this coming year.

During World War II there was a little mother left to care for her three children while her husband served in the armed forces. In the cold wet misery of winter two of the children became ill. The mother sat up all night bathing their heads with cool water and giving them medicine. Often during the night she prayed and asked God to heal her children and to take care of her husband until he could return home.

In the wee hours of the morning the children seemed to be better and were asleep. The weary mother walked to a window and looked out. There, high in the sky, she saw the morning star. The star looked very beautiful and yet very alone.

"You are like me, left alone," the mother spoke. She rested her head against the window, and tears of sorrow and fear fell from her eyes. Suddenly she looked up again at the star.

"You are shining on my husband also. Please tell him I am doing the best I can."

Months later, when the husband was home again and the family was getting reestablished, the mother told of her awful night when the children were so ill.

"That morning star often brought hope to us as we stood guard duty," the husband told her. "When we saw it in the heavens we took hope because we knew day was very near."

Sometimes as Christian workers we feel the way ahead is hopeless and discouraging. Remember we have been promised a morning star, our Lord and Saviour Jesus Christ. He is there all the time. He knows all our hardships and problems. Always he wants us to get the message, "Day is very near."

As the stars of this organization for this new year you will be expected to shine forth with hope and encouragement.

Napoleon was said to have faced a group of astrologers who were denying the fact of a God. He asked the question, "Gentlemen, who made these?" He pointed to the stars in the sky.

This organization will go forward in a great way because of the officer stars who will serve faithfully.

WORD TO THOSE WHO HAVE SERVED IN THE PAST:

Since this is a service for our whole church, it is a service where some change places of responsibility and a few stop to rest awhile. We would not want to go into our new year of work without saying a few words of appreciation to those who have been officers and teachers in the past.

You have served well, and we appreciate the good foundation you have laid for the new officers. Some of you are going on serving in the same places, others are making changes, but all will look to the great Morning Star of our faith and trust in him.

INSTALLATION OF OFFICERS:

(Have the pianist softly play, "Give of Your Best to the Master." As the music plays, have all the general officers of the Sunday School march to the front.)

General Officers

You are the guiding stars of our organization. Many times you will point the way to a discouraged teacher or worker. See that you are shining brightly in your place each Sunday.

(Pass to each one a silver star. Ask each to place his star on a large flannel board at the front. Reserve seats at the front for all officers to be installed. At the close, as the pianist plays "Onward, Christian Soldiers," let all the new officers march out.)

Superintendents

Have you ever looked into the heavens and been inspired by the beauty of the stars? As you lead your department this year, you are to inspire them to win new members. You are to have such good opening programs that they will go to class in a spirit of worship.

You must also see that classes have teachers if some teachers have to be absent. Yours is truly an important task, and the growth of your department rests upon your shoulders.

Departmental Officers

Your stars may not shine in such a prominent place as the stars of your leaders, but they are just as important. Without you, things would not run smoothly, and efficiency would be lost. It will be a joy to your pastor and superintendent to see you in your place each Sunday.

Teachers

It is said more people look for the galaxy called the Milky Way than for any constellation. So it is with teachers. You influence more people than anyone in our organization except the pastor. So you must ever keep your stars shining and bright. You will want to spend much time in preparation and prayer for your class.

They will look to see how your star is shining about many important issues in life.

Group Leaders

How we do like to see the sky when it is filled with many, many stars! Some are brighter than others, but all have a part in making the heavens beautiful.

The group leaders are many and are very important. The teacher, superintendent and pastor depend upon you to keep in touch with your individual group and to notify them when there is a need for a visit or other help.

PLEDGE OF OFFICERS:

Will all the officers stand as I read a pledge? When the pledge has been read, will you all promise to keep it by saying in unison, "I do"?

Will you promise to study the duties of your office and carry them out to the best of your abilities for the glory of God?

TO ALL OTHER MEMBERS PRESENT:

Are you an active member,
  The kind that would be missed,
Or are you just contented
  That your name is on the list?
Do you attend the meetings,
  And mingle with the flock,
Or do you stay at your office
  And criticize and knock?
Do you ever work on committees,
  To see there is no trick?
Or leave the work to just a few
  And talk about the clique?
So come to the meetings often,
  And help with hand and heart:
Don't be just a member
  But take an active part.

(AUTHOR UNKNOWN)

13

ATHLETIC INSTALLATION

Best Use:

For a club, group of young people or men.

Equipment Needed:

Tennis rackets, bats, footballs, basketballs, bowling ball, bow and arrow. All or a few of these may be used as decoration. If you have a banquet, cover the table with white paper, then cut streamers of colored crepe paper in the local school colors. Make small goalposts and place in the center of the table.

Cut small footballs or basketballs out of brown construction paper. These are to be given to each officer as he is installed. If you wish to have a menu or a program, cut in the shape of a football on a fold and place a program or menu inside.

If the organization has any trophies from the past, be sure to display these in a central place.

Scripture:

Use one of the following for each officer.

"I press toward the mark for the prize of the high calling of God in Christ Jesus" (Phil. 3:14).

"When thou goest, thy steps shall not be straitened; and when thou runnest, thou shalt not stumble" (Prov. 4:12).

"Let us lay aside every weight, and the sin which doth so easily beset us, and let us run with patience the race that is set before us" (Heb. 12:1).

(Phil. 2.16; 1 Cor. 1:9; Hab. 2:1-2; 1 Cor. 15:58.)

STORY:

John was just an average country boy. He lived on a small farm in East Texas. His great ambition was to become a ball player. About all the ball he knew anything about was baseball. The boys in the community often played on Saturday and Sunday afternoons.

John never could stay after school and play football because he must work on the farm. He would read all he could find about sports in the newspaper.

John finished school and went to a town to find work and attend college. He was just thrilled to death with the sports in the college, but again he must work in order to stay in school.

The day came when John was given a chance to play basketball. The coach, noticing how strong and agile he was, asked him why he didn't try out for the team and maybe a scholarship.

John was so nervous and excited he could not study the night before he was to try his luck.

What a wonderful afternoon for John as he caught the ball and as he threw goals! The coach felt he had made a real find. By this time next year he felt he would have John shaped into a real fine player.

For weeks John worked with all the strength he had to follow the instructions of his coach. He had never known such happiness and such a feeling of accomplishment.

While John was home working on the farm during the summer, his father died. There were three younger children and his mother to take care of. It was with a heavy heart he wrote his coach and told him he would not be able to return to school in the fall.

John's mother was sad that she had to be the cause of his dropping out of school.

"Sometimes the game of life hands us some bad breaks, Son, but we just have to accept them and keep fighting to win," she told her son.

John took a correspondence course at night and worked to keep his brother and sisters in high school. "Someday I'll go back to college," he promised himself.

One by one the younger children finished high school and found work in other places. At last John and his mother were left alone on the small farm.

One day, unexpectedly, all the family came home for a weekend. John was glad to see them. They were his family, and he loved them.

As they were gathered around the table eating, a knock came at the door. The lawyer from the small town nearby came in.

"John you have been such a good son to quit school and take care of all your family," his mother said, "now we are going to take care of you."

"What do you mean, Mother? I only did my duty," John said.

"We are signing these papers to give you this farm as a token of our gratitude. You may rent it or work it, but at least you know we appreciate what you did for us."

"Mother, you said yourself I only got some bad breaks in the game." John was stunned.

Soon John had rented the farm. With his mother to keep house for him, he went back to college. Because of his correspondence courses he soon finished school and found a job easier than farming.

After he was married, his two children turned out to be girls. But John and his wife decided they needed some ball players in the family, so they adopted two boys.

"Good breaks or bad I played the game as best I could and life has been good to me; not what I had dreamed but what was best for the whole team—my family. I am happy." So John could feel life had been a good game.

As you take your new offices, there will come times when you feel the breaks are bad. You must each try to serve to the best of your ability. Then you will be a winner.

CHARGE TO OFFICERS:

Teacher or Leader ——————, you are given the privilege of keeping this group fit. To keep fit they will need spiritual food, physical exercise, and a mental exercise in how to play the game of life.

Will you forget the games won in the past—or lost—and concentrate on making this a winning team?

Captain or President ——————, you are to set the pace for the spirit of this team. You may have to substitute for a teammate when there is a gap to be filled. You are a key man. You will lead by being thoughtful of other people's needs and desires. Lead your team to grow in Christian service.

Vice-president ——————, you will have the responsibility of the hits and runs of this group. You will help keep before the group the goal of life. When someone is in need of defense, you will be a triple threat to the enemy. Keep things running smoothly by obeying your captain's orders.

Secretary ————, you will be the quarterback. You will call off the "offensive signals" and direct the scoring plays on the football field. You will keep the group informed each meeting. If they are falling behind you will remind them to keep working.

Group Captains ————, all of you will be our blockers, our power men, our left ends, and right ends, to keep the game going. Without you we will lose the game. Hold the line and be in your places always.

Service

Some men are now trying to go to the moon;
The earth is so crowded they want to go soon;
   But while they sail off on a quest into space,
   Let us work at home on our own rocket race.

We will follow our orbit here in our hometown;
We will put on a smile that will wipe off the frown;
   Through our Sunday School class, let us serve here and there
   As we help people find their own happiness share.

For service to others will cause us to grow,
And we will rejoice, if as daily we go,
   We fulfil the need of the folk near at hand,
   While we serve our dear Lord as we live in this land.

J. T. BOLDING

(*Other organizations may be substituted for Sunday School class, for example, our department; Rotary Club; Odd Fellows Lodge; Masons group; own service club; own Garden Club.*)

14

VESSELS OF SERVICE

BEST USE:

For a men's or women's mission group, a class, or a club.

EQUIPMENT NEEDED:

Use as a central focal point a table with as many containers as there are officers to be installed. As you mention each officer, show the vessel representing him.

At a toy store, purchase a set of toy cooking utensils. Give one to each officer as he is installed.

If the above is too much trouble, use a flannel board or an easel. Cut pictures of different vessels from a magazine or a catalog and mount them on paper. As you talk, place one for each officer on the board.

SCRIPTURE:

"If a man therefore purge himself from these, he shall be a vessel unto honour, sanctified, and meet for the master's use, and prepared unto every good work" (2 Tim. 2:21).

STORY:

Joe and his wife Sarah were very happy in their new home. He had a good job, and they were expecting their first baby. Then Joe, a member of the Army Reserve, was called for active duty.

The young couple felt as if the world had fallen in on them. Their home must be sold, for a soldier's pay would not meet payments. Sarah must go and live with relatives. Their baby might be born while Joe was far away.

The two had always read the Scriptures together each night before retiring. On their last evening together the Scripture reading included Acts 9:15.

"But the Lord said unto him, Go thy way: for he is a chosen vessel unto me, to bear my name before the Gentiles, and kings, and the children of Israel."

"Joe, perhaps you are a chosen vessel," Sarah said as they sat talking. "There must be some work for you to do in the Army, or God would not have allowed this to happen."

"Sarah I promise I will live as clean and pure as I possibly can before the men I have to work with."

So Joe was sent to Korea, and Sarah went to her mother's. Life for both seemed bleak and unhappy.

Sarah felt she could not go through the birth of her child without the presence of her beloved husband. Just the day before the baby was born a letter came from Joe. At the close he wrote:

"Remember dear you are a chosen vessel to take care of our baby."

As Sarah was going through the pangs of childbirth she clutched in her mind the words, "You are a chosen vessel."

A few months later she wrote to her husband and reminded him that he, too, was "a chosen vessel to bear the Lord's name."

Joe had planned on his day off to go into town with

a group of his buddies and really have a ball. He was tired of being away from home. He felt cheated and hopeless.

As the boys were riding the army truck into the city, they passed a small building with a sign over the door, "Evangelical Mission."

When the truck stopped and the boys started toward a place they knew would serve strong drink and offer other pastimes, Joe stopped and turned away. Before his vision had passed the words from his wife's letter.

"You are a chosen vessel."

He wandered around among the shops, bought a few trinkets, and then walked back to the mission. Inside he met a missionary and was invited to eat a home-cooked meal.

That evening late, when they were back in camp, some of the boys asked Joe where he had disappeared. He told them about his visit to the mission. They laughed and jeered, but in a few weeks, when Joe was ordered home, some were heard to say, "It couldn't happen to a better guy."

CHARGE TO THE OFFICERS:

Each officer to be installed is a vessel for the Master's use.

President, here is the largest stewpan for you. You will need a large vessel full of patience and love if you are to lead this organization to greater heights.

Vice-president, here is a saucepan for your vessel. You will need to make a sauce of pride in your organization and ambition to fill in always when your president requires your help.

Secretary, a nice little teapot for you. The tea you will brew must be reheated at the next meeting each time. Keep the flavor pure and easy to digest.

Treasurer, for you, an important vessel, a skillet. Will you please see that tempers never burn over a lack of proper reports on the financial standing of this organization?

Group leaders (*use plastic or toy knives and forks and spoons*), for you a place setting of tableware. You will be working with a group of people. Just as each knife, fork, and spoon serves a purpose, so you must keep close watch on each member of your group for each person is a vessel unto honor for the Master's use.

Teacher, for you we have a lovely mixing bowl. The others have the work of carrying on the organization but to you we leave the serving of the lessons.

The Human Touch

It's just the little human touch
   That makes the game worthwhile,
The little helpful words of praise,
   The small and cheery smile.

Though success crown your efforts and
   You're near the higher peak
The Lord be thanked for kindly words
   Men did not fear to speak.

When troubles daunt and sorrows sway,
   And all the world is wrong,
When sunshine is obscured by rain,
   And silent is all song,
It's mighty hard to pull ahead
   When hope is almost gone.

But little words like these have helped—
  "Good work, old man, keep on!"
It does not take much time to say
  A word or two of praise,
And yet uncounted worth is there
  To help through cheerless days.

And oh, the hearts that have gained hope
  When life was drear and bleak,
From the kindly words, and cheering words
  Men did not fear to speak.

(AUTHOR UNKNOWN)

PRAYER:

Lord, make each officer a vessel unto honor in thy service. Encourage them when they are discouraged, and make all to rejoice with them when there is success and growth.

May each officer strive to keep his vessel of service brightly polished and ready for use.

15

RAINBOW OF COLORS

BEST USE:

Ladies' mission organization or club. Good for young women of any age. Not very suitable for men or boys.

EQUIPMENT NEEDED:

If this service can be held in the evening, ask the ones to be installed to wear pastel evening clothes.

Prepare a rainbow out of many colors of ribbon or crepe paper. Let the rainbow come down to a pot of gold. This pot may be a brass- or gold-colored container. If one is not available, cover a large punch bowl with gold foil.

Cut small pots out of gold construction paper. Have one to hand each member as she is installed. On the back may be written or pasted the duties of the officer. The handles of the pots may be cut out and a ribbon tied in the opening.

SCRIPTURE:

"I do set my bow in the cloud, and it shall be for a token of a covenant between me and the earth" (Gen. 9:13).

STORY:

During the depression a family of five moved from the sandy land of Southeastern Oklahoma to the blackland belt of Texas. Just a day after they arrived at their new home rains started. For ten days it rained. The family was accustomed to going right on in the rain, but one trip out in the black mud made them realize things were different in North Texas. The children cried, the mother cried, and the father felt like crying because he was not getting to work.

Late one afternoon the father came in from the barn and asked all the family to come to the back porch.

"Look there in the sky." He pointed to a beautiful rainbow. "The rains will be over tomorrow."

"Look in the West," the children cried. "There is the sun peeping out."

So the little family learned that no matter how sticky the mud and how long the rain, there would always come a day of glorious sunshine.

As new officers you may at times feel overwhelmed with the problems and the trials of getting a new year started, but soon all will be smooth sailing, and you will be glad you took a responsibility.

CHARGE TO OFFICERS:

(The charge is for different colors. The installing officer can fit them to the list of officers she has to instal. If it works out, the colors might match the dresses the women or girls are wearing.)

RED. This color in our modern world usually means "stop." Stop is a good thing for you to do. Stop and realize your great responsibility as ————— of this group. The bright color of red shows your brilliant plans for making this a happy successful year.

GREEN. In today's world, green always means "go." Go you must if you are to keep this organization growing and lively. Green is one of the most restful colors for the eyes, but there will be no rest for you as you keep going as ———————— of this group.

YELLOW. Yellow reminds us of gold, and gold is precious to all people. Yours is a precious opportunity to shine as you direct the programs. You will lead in spreading knowledge and understanding as you serve as ———————— for the group.

INDIGO. This color is not brilliant and showy, but it is important in any color scheme of the fine artist. You will not create a lot of attention as you carry on the quiet duties of ————————, but, remember, you help make the picture beautiful and complete.

ORANGE. Oranges make us think of something good to eat and sweet to the taste. Your socials as you plan them will be sweet to remember.

VIOLET. There must always be one color which is dainty and lovely. Violet makes us think of the beauty of spring. As ———————— you will see that the meetings are well advertised and your reports will be a high color in each meeting.

BLUE. A blue flame is the flame of intense heat. Your enthusiasm will be the blue flame keeping this group burning with zeal. Zeal for the projects and purposes of our organization.

Red, green, yellow, indigo, orange, violet, and blue, all such lovely ladies, such lovely colors, blending together they will make a thing of beauty and harmony for all to see. Carry out your responsibilities and keep your colors bright. Then your pot of gold will truly be found.

The Rainbow with the Rain

Tho' the stormy clouds may hover o'er me,
　And life is burdened with sorrow's pain,
Christ my Pilot ever goes before me,
　He sends the rainbow with the rain. . . .

He sends the rainbow, a lovely rainbow,
　He sends the rainbow with the rain;
He sends the sunshine upon the shadow,
　He sends the rainbow with the rain.

B. B. McKinney

16

SANDS OF TIME

BEST USE:

For any type group elected for a one-year period of time.

EQUIPMENT NEEDED:

If possible, secure enough small, cheap, three-minute egg timers for each officer to be installed. If it is too expensive to buy the egg timers, use black and white construction paper and paste up small replicas on cards. Write on each one the name of the officer and hand it to the one being installed.

For an interest center, use a large clock surrounded by as many clocks as possible. They do not have to be running although it is more effective if they are.

If the above is not possible, make a large cardboard clock face with hands fastened on a screw. Put the face of the clock on a flannel board and, as each officer is installed, turn the hand slowly around one time.

SCRIPTURE:

"Remember how short my time is: wherefore hast thou made all men in vain?" (Psalm 89:47).

"To every thing there is a season, and a time to every purpose under the heaven: A time to be born, and a time to die; a time to plant, and a time to pluck up that which is planted" (Eccl. 3:1-2).

"A time to keep silence, and a time to speak" (Eccl. 3:7).

POEM:

> Time, you old gypsy man,
>   Will you not stay,
> Put up your caravan
> Just for one day?

RALPH HODGSON

STORY:

There had been a great uprising in the high school, and many pupils had followed the crowd and gotten into trouble. Now many of the students stood to lose their credits for the year's work.

"Old Owl Eyes," as the pupils called the principal, did not want this to happen. Yet, he could not ignore the fact that the students had broken a lot of rules. They had been defiant and destructive. How could he restore peace and cooperation in the school without losing face or making the pupils lose too much esteem for themselves?

After much worry and prayer, the principal went to a hobby shop and asked for a candle that would burn for eight hours. This candle he placed in the glass window of his office. Before lighting it, he had a large number of handbills passed out. The handbills stated:

At eight o'clock in the morning this candle in my window will be lighted. Any pupil who has been expelled from school will be reinstated if he comes to my office and signs a school loyalty pledge before the candle burns out. After it has gone out I will make the expulsion permanent for those who have not signed the pledge and agreed to act as high school boys and girls should act.

YOUR PRINCIPAL

At eight the next morning the candle was lighted and made a small flame in the office window. The pupils came in one by one at first. As the day wore on and the candle grew smaller, they came by two's and three's. Still, some of the most unruly had not been in by afternoon. Only a short time was left of the eight hours.

The principal was very anxious to make the list complete and clear up the trouble. He asked his secretary to print another handbill and have it passed out as school was being dismissed for the day.

It read:

Every great offer has its candle of limitations. You have only a few hours left to show your loyalty to your school. There is only one high school in our town. If you fail to make use of your opportunity to attend it, you will find someday time has run out on the jobs you can get and the society you can fit. Do not let the candle burn out before you come to my office.

YOUR PRINCIPAL

At 4 o'clock, just as the candle began to flicker, the last bit of wick in a pool of oil, the door opened and the last of the young people came in. As they were signing the loyalty pledge, the flame sputtered and went out.

"We just made it!" they cried as the principal put his arms around them and talked.

"Boys, we want only what is good for you. Next time

there might not be a candle. Let's make this a good school."

There is a limited period of time for the officers of this organization to make it a good and powerful one. You may think your task is the hardest one in the class. Remember as someone has written long ago: "Anyone can carry his burden, however heavy, till nightfall. Anyone can do his work, however hard, for one day. Anyone can live sweetly, patiently, lovingly, purely, till the sun goes down. And this is all that life ever really means."

CHARGE TO OFFICERS:

President. —————, your time will be filled with seeing that the others do not let their time run out without fulfilling their allotted task.

Think of yourself as one holding a timer in your hand and you must have unparalleled success before the sands of this year's time run out. A glorious year lies ahead of you. Achieve, achieve for the best organization ever.

Vice-president. —————, your timer is to remind you that you cannot be and not be at the same time. If you serve faithfully in your allotted place you cannot lose. Honest service cannot come to loss. Your sands of time will run out as fast as your president's. Be sure you serve well.

Secretary. —————, your time is well spent at each meeting as you keep records. Yours will be the splendor of beauty, the beauty of well-kept notes and minutes.

Group Leaders. —————, I would say to all of you, have a plan! Cooperate, and feel it a privilege to hold an office.

Life

God gives us each but one short day
  The time that we call life—
To waste or cherish as we will,
  To spend in peace or strife;
One little day in which to do,
  Or else to leave undone,
The work he gives us: we must leave
  It all at set of sun.

But one brief day! Oh, help me Lord
  To use it as I should!
Help me, for others in that day
  To do some little good.
And when at twilight cool and dim,
  I hear thy gentle call,
Dear Lord, forgive me, if for thee
  I've not used time and all.

(AUTHOR UNKNOWN)

CLOSING WORDS:

Henry Ward Beecher wrote: "As ships meet at sea, a moment together, when words of greeting must be spoken, and then away into the deep, so men meet in this world; and I think we should cross no man's path without hailing him, and, if needs be, giving him supplies."

As officers you have met for this period of time to serve together. May you work together and help each other before your time runs out on your period of service.

17

FLYING ON

This installation is primarily for adult classes or clubs. It can be adapted to departments or children's groups.

EQUIPMENT NEEDED:

For each officer, make paper airplanes from colored construction paper, or buy cheap little plastic planes at a variety store. Write your state Sunday School department and ask for enough free leaflets for the officers of the age group you are installing. (Example: "The Adult Bible Class at Work.")

As each officer is installed, give him one of the leaflets. If you use paper planes, pin one on their shoulder. If toy planes are used, put a string on each one long enough to go around the officer's neck.

Decorate the room with model airplanes, if they can be borrowed.

SCRIPTURE:

"Ye have seen what I did unto the Egyptians, and how I bare you on eagles' wings, and brought you unto myself" (Ex. 19:4).

"Be merciful unto me, O God, be merciful unto me: for

my soul trusteth in thee: yea in the shadow of thy wings will I make my refuge, until these calamities be overpast" (Psalm 57:1).

STORY:

A few years ago, when people were flocking to Alaska hoping to find free land and a fresh start in life, the Bowen family made the long trip in a trailer.

The land was found, and they prepared for a winter of hardship in order to get started. Nothing had prepared them for a life without television, without a school close by, and without a supermarket for shopping.

The school problem was worked out by Mother and Daddy teaching the children from books ordered from New York. The radio helped keep them in touch with the outside world. But, in all their dreaming of a home and land of their own, they had not realized there would be times when they could not leave home and go the ten miles into the village because of snow.

There came the day when they awoke to find their trailer home almost covered with snow. They could not keep warm without staying as close to the stove as possible.

"What will we do?" Mother cried. "Our food will run out before we can get out to go to town."

As the days went along, it seemed that the family would indeed be hungry before there was a chance for food. There were no phones and no way of communication.

About noon one day, when they had just about given up hope, there was the roar of a plane overhead.

Father grabbed his coat and warm cap and rushed outside. For a moment he could not think how to signal their need.

Then he thought of the woodpile he had cleared of snow that morning.

He began laying sticks of wood to form a huge word "food." The plane flew away, but in a few hours it was back and dropped a large package of food near the trailer.

So the Bowen family made their first winter in the Alaskan wilderness. The next year they would know better how to prepare for the problems of the North.

CHARGE TO OFFICERS:

New officers will meet unexpected problems their first term of office. Do not be afraid. There will be someone who has been an officer before who will keep you from failing. Don't be afraid to ask questions and take advice.

President. You will fly a plane of leadership. Your plane will have the fuel of understanding. The stops will be made with wisdom. Yours is the largest of all planes. We might call it the latest jet. Let leadership ever keep flying on.

Vice-president. You will fly the plane of assistance. You will fill it with the fuel of helpfulness. Invitation and enlistment will be the fare served on your plane. The plane of assistance is not the largest one made, but it is very important to keep it flying on.

Secretary. You will fly a plane capable of skywriting. Your words must be dependable and accurate. Write well and keep flying on.

Treasurer. Your plane is the treasure plane. You will never be too heavily loaded in this organization, but fly well with what is entrusted to your care.

Program Chairman. Your plane will be one of bright colors and interesting programs. The fuel will be information and planning. I hope you fly so well that your last program is as interesting as the first one.

Mission Study. You fly the plane called "facts," facts about the work and needs in our mission fields. You will fill your plane with challenge and see that each member hears the roar of your engines.

Prayer. Your plane is one we all admire for it is flown with a halo of holiness around it. Yet, it must run on the fuel of dedication and consecration. You will remain humble as you keep flying on.

Benevolence. You will fly in a helicopter, for you will need to touch down all over our city with gifts of compassion and words of encouragement and love. You will lead all your group in caring for those in need. Some will need physical things, but others will need spiritual leadership.

Stewardship. Your plane will be called "The Plane of Obedience." You will lead people to obey the command to "Bring ye all the tithes into the storehouse."

Youth Workers. Your plane will be called "Counsel and Hope." You will counsel the youth, lead them into great plans for the future. Cheer them with the knowledge that they can make the world better if they try hard enough. Encourage them to keep flying on.

Publicity. Your plane will have eye appeal. You will tell the story of your organization and make it so interesting others will want to join and members will not fail to attend.

Social. Your plane is the plane of fellowship. When you land it will be to make others happy and welcome.

DEDICATION POEM:

Be Listening

Among the things that this day brings,
   Will come to you a call,
To which, unless you're listening,
   You may not hear at all.
Lest it be very soft and low,
   Whate'er you do, where'er you go,
   Be listening!

Then whatsoe'er the call may be,
   To service small or great,
To cross the seas and speak God's love,
   To smile, to rule a state—
When God shall come and say to you,
"Here is the thing that you must do,"
   Be listening!

(AUTHOR UNKNOWN)

18

CLIMBING STEPS OF SERVICE

BEST USE:

For large groups or small, depending on how elaborate you wish to be. The officers listed are officers that might be in almost any organization of men or women. Other officers might be added. Use the extra steps mentioned.

EQUIPMENT NEEDED:

Cut two pieces of styrofoam into staircase shape. Place other pieces of styrofoam across the pieces to form steps. Cover this with wallpaper or contact paper to look like stairs which are carpeted.

The same effect can be had with a tall cardboard box. Cut the sides and use other pieces of cardboard across to make the stairs. Cover this with any kind of paper that can be glued on to make the steps look attractive.

The steps should be about three feet tall overall. Each one should be about three or four inches higher than the one below.

Write out the names of the officers for use on the steps as each officer is installed.

Place a cross behind the steps and towering above it. At the foot of the cross use a long cardboard poster with these words printed on it: "Ye serve the Lord Christ" (Col. 3:24).

From a strip of crepe paper or butcher paper make a

pathway leading to the bottom of the steps. Shine spotlight, preferably colored, on the interest center.

SCRIPTURE:

"Doth not he see my ways, and count all my steps?" (Job 31:4).

"The steps of a good man are ordered by the Lord: and he delighteth in his way" (Psalm 37:23).

"Righteousness shall go before him; and shall set us in the way of his steps" (Psalm 85:13).

POEM:

Be a Man

It takes a little courage,
 And a little self-control,
And some grim determination,
 If you want to reach a goal.
It takes a deal of striving,
 And a firm and stern-set chin,
No matter what the battle,
 If you're really out to win.

There's no easy path to glory,
 There's no rosy road to fame;
Life, however we may view it,
 Is no simple parlor game;
But its prizes call for fighting,
 For endurance and for grit,
For a rugged disposition,
 And a "don't-know-when-to-quit."

(AUTHOR UNKNOWN)

STORY:

Since the early history of mankind, people have been building steps. They started with the man who wanted to climb to the top of a steep bluff and thus cut out crude steps in the rocky wall. Steps have progressed until today there are wonderful escalators which take a man up and up as he stands on a step.

A stairway must have a goal in view to be worth the building. Most of us know about plain steps which lead up and into our homes, or steps which take us up to the second story of our home.

A stairway must have a strong foundation so that people will trust it to hold them up as they climb.

One of our dearly beloved presidents of the nation, practiced pulling himself up the steps of his home after he had been a victim of polio. He reached the top, not only of the steps but of our national leadership.

There will be steps for you as officers to climb as you serve this year. You will at times feel that the goal is too hard to reach. At times you will want to stop climbing and slide down, but you must strive for the goal—the goal of doing your very best for your organization.

If you feel several others have a higher position on the steps than you, just remember you are on the way up and are important in your elected place.

CHARGE TO OFFICERS:

"Let us rise up and build" (Neh. 2:18).

President. You are charged with the responsibility of leading your officers up these steps. You are to build a bigger, better, more beautiful organization than has been known before. You will not stand on steps of brick, stone, or wood. You will climb spiritual steps. You will seek to build the character of the officers who serve with you.

(*Place a card which reads,* "Organized forces," *on the first step of your styrofoam steps.*)

President, you will stand on the step of organized forces.

Vice-president. You will stand on the step called "Readiness," for you will at all times be ready to help your leader. See that no stumbling blocks have been left on the steps as your organization seeks to climb to spiritual heights.

Secretary. You will stand on the step called "Accuracy," for the records you keep must be concise and clear. They are important and the whole stairway depends upon them.

Treasurer. You stand on a step of "Caution," caution for the care of the funds entrusted to your care.

Program Leader. You will stand on the step labeled "Interest." You will seek to make your programs different and interesting to all who participate.

Chorister. You will ever stand on the step labeled "Joyful Noise." You will lead the group to make a joyful noise unto the Lord.

Pianist. Your step is the step of "Harmony." Your lovely rendition of the music will help make the programs more inspiring and helpful.

Publicity Chairman. At the top step we find "Propaganda." You will see that the news is told about your organization. You will make it so interesting and exciting people will not want to miss a meeting.

CLOSING:

So you will all climb the steps of service, helping each other, and making the whole a beautiful sight.

May God bless and keep each of you as you stand on your step of service. How empty the stairs will look if you fail to fill your places!

19

SCALES OF SERVICE

BEST USE:

Can be used for an adult department or a class in an older group of teenagers, young adults, or for a club.

EQUIPMENT NEEDED:

Place the largest picture of Christ you have available on a center table. Open a large Bible and elevate it at the lower part of the picture. Place a pair of scales to one side. The ornamental kind found in so many homes today will be very attractive.

On a small piece of cardboard write or print the letters, "A Fruitful, Successful Year." Place this on one side of the scales after you have told the lead-up story. As each officer's name is called, place a small cardboard on the opposite side of the scales, the point being that the scales will be balanced when all officers are in their places. To be sure of balancing you can take two identical pieces of cardboard. Use one on the organization side, the other cut into the same number of pieces as you have officers.

SCRIPTURE:

"How beautiful upon the mountains are the feet of him that bringeth good tidings, that publisheth peace; that bringeth good tidings of good, that publisheth salvation; that saith unto Zion, Thy God reigneth!" (Isa. 52:7).

STORY:

As a department you are marching into a new year, a new era. Many of your pupils are new and have new rooms. What a privilege to be able to advance each year, to see new people, to meet new leaders!

Our world is one torn often with strife. People think first of themselves and their own gain. I charge you, as an officer in this group for the coming year, to venture from your own selfish shoreline and seek to balance the scales for good.

These scales are not very important as far as weighing anything goes, but we serve one "who hath measured the waters in the hollow of his hand, and meted out heaven with the span, and comprehended the dust of the earth in a measure, and weighed the mountains in scales, and the hills in a balance" (Isa. 40:12).

A few years ago, when farmers were still allowing their children to pick the cotton, a certain farmer promised his children a trip to town and some money to spend on Saturday if they would work hard and finish picking a bale.

The three children were very anxious for the day off and the trip to town. Their father allowed them to weigh their own cotton sacks each time they were full and to write the amount down on a sheet of paper. The oldest was so afraid they would not finish the bale and get to go to town he resorted to crooked tactics.

Each time he went to write his weight on the paper he made it five pounds more than it really was. The father was surprised that the bale was going so fast. He usually wanted a bale to weigh five hundred pounds when it was ginned.

On Friday afternoon the figures showed there was plenty of cotton in the trailer for a good bale. The children were assured of a trip to town next day.

"We will go early and get the cotton ginned," the father said. "Then I will sell it and give each of you some money."

When the cotton was ginned, the bale lacked twenty-five pounds weighing as much as it should have. The father was very disappointed, but he kept his promise to the children and let them spend some money.

"Something must be wrong with our scales," he told the children on the way home.

The next week the father weighed all the sacks, and he noticed that his oldest child was picking lots less than the records showed he had picked the week before.

When questioned, the boy confessed his guilt and asked his father to forgive him.

If you as officers fail to carry your share of the load in this organization the scales will be unbalanced.

CHARGE TO OFFICERS:

Will all the departmental officers stand? As officers starting a new year, look at the scales. They will not balance if you are absent, if you fail to carry out the task assigned to you. With Edward Everett Hale you might say:

> I am only one,
> But still I am one.
> I cannot do everything,
> But still I can do something;
> And because I cannot do everything
> I will not refuse to do the something that I can do.

Will all the teachers stand? For scales to be accurate there must be some weights on one side. You are the most important weights on the scales. You give direction and purpose to the classes you teach. See that the scales of service do not get out of balance because you are absent or uninterested.

It Isn't the Church—It's You[1]

When everything seems to be going wrong,
    And trouble seems everywhere brewing;
When prayer meeting, Young People's meeting, and all,
    Seems simmering slowly—stewing,
Just take a look at yourself and say,
    "What's the use of being blue?"
Are you doing your "bit" to make things "hit"?
    It isn't the church—it's *you*.

It's really strange sometimes, don't you know,
    That things go as well as they do,
When we think of the little—the very small mite—
    We add to the work of the few.
We sit, and stand round, and complain of what's done,
    And do very little but fuss.
Are we bearing our share of the burdens to bear?
    It isn't the church—it's *us*.

So, if you want to have the kind of a church
    Like the kind of a church you like,
Put off your guile, and put on your best smile,
    And hike, my brother, just hike,
To the work in hand that has to be done—
    The work of saving a few.
It isn't the church that is wrong, my boy;
    It isn't the church—it's *you*.

JAMES GILCHRIST LAWSON

1. James Gilchrist Lawson, "It Isn't the Church—It's You," *World's Best-Loved Poems* (New York: Harper & Bros., 1927.)

20

GARDEN PARTY

BEST USE:

For women's or girls' organizations.

EQUIPMENT NEEDED:

A vase of real or artificial flowers. Have plenty. They will not all be used, but they will help make the interest center attractive. Use a sheet of styrofoam on a table with some green cloth or crepe paper to make an attractive decoration in front of the sheet. A low white fence made from white cardboard can be placed around the styrofoam leaving an opening for a gate. This sheet is your garden. As you install each officer you place a flower for that officer in the garden. (Artificial flowers with stiff wire stems will stick into the foam best.)

SCRIPTURE:

"The Lord shall guide thee continually, and satisfy thy soul in drought, and make fat thy bones: and thou shalt be like a watered garden, and like a spring of water, whose waters fail not" (Isa. 58:11).

Poem:

The Watered Lilies

The Master stood in his garden,
    Among the lilies fair,
Which his own right hand had planted
    And trained with tenderest care.

. . . .
"My lilies need to be watered,"
    The heavenly Master said;
"Wherein shall I draw it for them,
    And raise each drooping head?"

Close to his feet on the pathway,
    Empty, and frail, and small,
An earthen vessel was lying,
    Which seemed of no use at all;

But the Master saw, and raised it
    From the dust in which it lay,
And smiled, as he gently whispered:
    "This shall do my work to-day:

"It is but an earthen vessel,
    But it lay so close to me;
It is small, but it is empty,
    And that is all it needs to be."

So to the fountain he took it,
    And filled it full to the brim;
How glad was the earthen vessel
    To be of some use to him!

. . . .
He watered the drooping lilies
    Until they revived again.

And the Master saw, with pleasure,
That his labor was not in vain.

His own hand had drawn the water
Which refreshed the thirsty flowers,
But he used the earthen vessel
To convey the living showers.

And to itself it whispered,
As he laid it aside once more.
"Still will I lie in His pathway,
Just where I did before.

"Close would I keep to the Master,
Empty would I remain,
And some day He may use me
To water His flowers again."

(AUTHOR UNKNOWN)

CHARGE TO OFFICERS:

I will choose for our *president-elect* the tallest flower in the bouquet and plant it in the garden of service. (*Take a tall flower out of vase and stick it into the styrofoam garden.*)

Our president, like this flower, must stand straight and tall above the other officers. You must be able to look about at the others and see their possibilities. Inspire them to grow as best they can.

Vice-president, your flower is not as tall as that of the president, but it is very similar in nature. You make the garden beautiful because you cooperate so well with your leader.

Secretary, you will be represented by some flowers often called ground cover, yet without them the garden is not half so pretty. Your place is important in making the garden smooth and lovely. You quietly keep notes and read them back again each meeting. This ground cover is always lovely. At times it blooms brightly, while at other times it is just a profusion of green leaves.

Treasurer, for you we have a lovely red rose. You are someone seen but not too often heard. You are necessary to make any garden bright and colorful.

Social chairman, you are like the daisy. You will not tell until the proper time just what fun and fellowship you have planned for our group. For you we place daisies of several colors in the garden. We use different colors to represent the variety of social events you will plan for us this year.

Publications director, for you we have a sweet smelling gardenia. Your publicity will spread out for many to read and enjoy, just as the aroma of the gardenia spreads.

Music committee, we will place some vines in the garden. They will twine about and make all the garden brighter and more attractive.

(*Place all the flowers left in the vase in the garden. They will represent the general membership, necessary to fill a garden with beauty.*)

DEDICATION:

Father, make each officer and each member like a beautiful flower as all seek to serve this year.

21

ESCALATOR OF EFFICIENCY

BEST USE:

For a small class or group.

EQUIPMENT NEEDED:

Use a flannel board and put the officers' names on it as they are installed. If a flannel board is not handy, use a large poster board on an easel and have the different officers' names covered with a blank strip of paper fastened on with transparent tape. As each officer is called, remove the blank paper and reveal his name.

Cut paper dolls out of a magazine and paste one above the other slantwise across the poster. Leave room at the feet of each for the step each is to stand on. Some of the steps may be: Word of God (for teacher), Leadership (for president), Efficiency (for vice-president), Accuracy (for secretary), Trust (for treasurer), Faithfulness (for group captains), Cooperation (for all members in general).

Place at the base of the escalator a piece of brown construction paper shaped like a rock. On this print "CHRIST."

SCRIPTURE:

"And he dreamed, and behold a ladder set up on the earth, and the top of it reached to heaven: and behold the angels of God ascending and descending on it" (Gen. 28:12).

STORY:

A man and his small daughter were going shopping. They stepped on the escalator in a large department store and were carried upward. At the top, when the child stepped off, she fell through an opening and was killed. Some workman had failed to put an "out of order" sign at the bottom.

A class cannot be efficient if every officer is not in his place and cooperating with the plans of the group.

God's work is the most important thing in our world. We should feel honored when we are given a place to fill. This class will not grow by accident, but by each officer standing in his place.

Christ is the rock on which we must base our escalator of efficiency.

The Solid Rock

My hope is built on nothing less
    Than Jesus' blood and righteousness;
I dare not trust the sweetest frame,
    But wholly lean on Jesus' name.

On Christ the solid Rock, I stand;
    All other ground is sinking sand,
All other ground is sinking sand.

EDWARD MOTE

Will all the officers come and stand facing the group?

CHARGE TO OFFICERS:

Teacher —————, you will often need to be reminded of the verse, "Study to shew thyself approved unto God, a workman that needeth not to be ashamed, rightly dividing the word of truth" (2 Tim. 2:15). You will stand on the "Word of God." You must be filled with a desire to impart this Word to your pupils. (*Place "Word of God" on the step, or, if covered, remove the cover.*)

President —————, you are charged with the responsibility of leadership. You are to take as much as possible from the shoulders of the teacher. You will see that the machinery of the class runs smoothly. "Teach me thy way, O Lord, and lead me in a plain path, because of mine enemies" (Psalm 27:11). (*Uncover the step called "Leadership."*)

Vice-president —————, you stand on one of the very vital steps on the escalator. Your responsibility is to seek new members and thus enlarge the class.

"Go ye therefore, and teach all nations" (Matt. 28:19). (*Uncover the step "Enlargement."*)

Group Leaders ————— [*Call names*] —————, look what a terrible gap would result on our escalator of efficiency if you did not stand in your proper places. You as group leaders are responsible for your group. If they are ill you visit them, if they are absent you find out why and get them back. "And let us not be weary in well-doing: for in due season we shall reap, if we faint not" (Gal. 6:9). (*Uncover the steps saying "Faithfulness, Enlistment, Visitation."*)

Secretary —————, you have been selected because you are an accurate person. You will keep neat and accurate records. "Let all things be done decently and in order" (1 Cor. 14:40). (*Uncover step with word "Accuracy."*)

Remaining class members—You are to cooperate with the officers you have elected. Unless you cooperate the machinery will stop and the escalator will never reach the top in efficiency.

POEM:

Chosen Ones

As I sat alone in my room one day,
I heard a small voice that seemed to say;
"I have chosen you to help with my work,
For there is much to do on my great earth.
Good helpers I need of every kind,
And I'm glad I found you just at this time."

(AUTHOR UNKNOWN)

Father, bless each member of this officer's cabinet and bless each class member for all are important in the kingdom work.

22

ROYAL ROAD TO READINESS

For a class of men or a club consisting of men.

EQUIPMENT NEEDED:

A large piece of clean newspaper tacked on a board and a small package of colored chalk.

As the leader talks, he can draw the road to readiness, or he can ask someone else to draw as he talks. Make a scene with a road in the center and perhaps a hill at the end of the road with three crosses on it. The drawing can be as elaborate as the talent of the artist permits. It can be very simple if necessary.

SCRIPTURE:

"And Achish said, Whither have ye made a road today?" (1 Sam. 27:10).

STORY:

An ancient story tells of a king in a poor country who sent out messengers to all parts of his kingdom. A prize would be given to the one who traveled best on the Royal Road of

Readiness. Lookouts were stationed all along the road. (*Have a road drawn on the white newspaper.*)

On the set day, people from all over the land started to travel toward the palace. Some sold all they had and bought fine chariots in which to travel. Others felt the king would want people to walk, but they must be dressed in fine clothes. So they bought gay apparel. (*Draw a cart on the road and some stick figures walking.*)

Begart lived in the very farthest corner of the realm. He was humble and poor so he had no thought of entering the race for the prize, but he wanted to see the crowd and have part in the excitement.

As Begart walked along the road watching the people in fine clothes, on horses, in chariots go by, he noticed a large stone in the center of the road. Running out, he grabbed up the stone and moved it out of the way. A cart almost hit him as he stooped to pick it up.

Farther along toward the palace, a small child broke away from his mother's hand and darted into the road. Begart ran for the child and snatched it up just as a fast-galloping horse went by.

It was well past noon when Begart could see the palace in the distance. He decided to stop and eat some of the lunch he was carrying. In the shade of a tree he sat quietly chewing his bread and drinking from a goatskin bottle. He noticed an old woman watching him with a hungry look in her eye.

"Here, take some of my bread." He offered her all he had left.

At last the race was over and the people gathered in front of the palace to hear the king award the prize.

"Will the peasant Begart come forward?"

Begart trembled with fear. What had he done except walk along and watch the people as they traveled?

"Begart, to you goes the prize for traveling the Royal Road best." The king handed him a pouch filled with gold.

"Oh, no, sir! I am only an onlooker. I had no money for a horse or fine clothes."

"Begart, you traveled best because you sought to make the road safe for others. Your trip has been a trip of service, therefore you traveled best."

CHARGE TO OFFICERS:

By now the artist has put trees and flowers along the road in the picture and off at a distance a faint outline of a castle. Ask all officers to stand. Read the following hymn.

O Master, Let Me Walk with Thee

O Master, let me walk with Thee
In lowly paths of service free;
Tell me Thy secret; help me bear
The strain of toil, the fret of care.

Help me the slow of heart to move
By some clear, winning word of love;
Teach me the wayward feet to stay,
And guide them in the homeward way.

Teach me Thy patience; still with Thee
In closer, dearer company,
In work that keeps faith sweet and strong,
In trust that triumphs over wrong.

In hope that sends a shining ray
Far down the future's broad'ning way,

In peace that only Thou canst give,
With thee, O Master, let me live.

WASHINGTON GLADDEN

CLOSING:

Ask all present to join in singing a verse of "Mine Eyes
Have Seen the Glory."

Mine eyes have seen the glory of the coming of the Lord;
He is trampling out the vintage where the grapes of wrath are
    stored;
He hath loosed the fateful lightning of His terrible swift sword,
His truth is marching on.

Glory! glory, hallelujah!
Glory! glory, hallelujah!
Glory! glory, hallelujah!
Our God is marching on.

JULIA WARD HOWE

23

BIBLE INSTALLATION

BEST USE:

For any age old enough to read and love the Bible.

EQUIPMENT NEEDED:

Write ahead to the American Bible Society, 450 Park Avenue, New York, New York, 10022. Ask for free literature on the Bible and Bible reading to pass out.

Arrange a table at the focal point of interest. Place, standing up on the table, as many copies of different versions of the Bible as the table will hold. American Bible Society may send a large poster. Mount this and stand it behind the Bibles.

SCRIPTURE:

"Thy word have I hid in mine heart, that I might not sin against thee" (Psalm 119:11).

STORY:

A mountain philosopher said: "A feller can't no more explain what he don't know than he can come back from where he ain't been." Most of you are better Bible students than I am, but I want us to talk about our new year's officers in the light of our love for the Book of Books and its author.

> I am my neighbor's Bible;
>   He reads me when we meet;
> Today he reads me in my home;
>   Tomorrow, in the street.
> He may be relative or friend,
>   Or slight acquaintance be;
> He may not even know my name;
>   Yet he is reading me.
> Dear Christian friends and brothers,
>   If we could only know
> How faithfully the world records
>   Just what we say and do
> Oh! we would make our record plain
>   And labor hard to see,
> Our world neighbors won to Christ,
>   While reading you and me!

(AUTHOR UNKNOWN)

I hold in my hand (*holds up Bible*) the most remarkable book in the world. There are more copies of this book in the world than of any other single book. This book is really a collection of a number of books, thirty-nine in the Old Testament and twenty-seven in the New Testament. Between thirty-five and forty authors labored over a period of fifteen hundred years to write the book. This book has been translated into almost one thousand different languages and dialects.

Men love the Word of God and probe its pages to seek its wisdom and truth.

Will all the newly-elected officers rise?

As you stand before us today, I would ask you to take the

Bible as your guide for leadership this year. In its pages you will find the solution for any problem you may face. Take time to read some each day. If possible, commit some verses to memory.

The Bible is filled with many wonderful promises but in closing I would read one: "If ye abide in me, and my words abide in you, ye shall ask what ye will, and it shall be done unto you" (John 15:7).

Bible Study

"Oh, not for wealth, nor fame, nor power,
  Nor love nor truest friend,
Would I forgo the sacred hour
  Which o'er God's Word I spend.
I steal it from the hours of sleep,
  If leisure be not given,
For only this the soul can keep
  In touch with God and heaven."

(AUTHOR UNKNOWN)

24

JEWEL BOX

For organizations consisting of women or girls. Young women especially enjoy this installation.

Equipment Needed:

If you have a pretty jewelry box available, use it to hold the jewels. If a bought jewelry box is not available, make one. Take a nice-sized cardboard box. Cut all kinds of colorful pictures out of magazines and paste them all over the box. They need to overlap and be in all sizes and shapes. When the box is covered with pictures and as attractive as you can make it, put a coat of shellac over it to give an antique effect.

Fill the jewel box with all kinds of costume jewelry. If you can find some that is not too expensive, just give it to each officer. If not, ask them to return it after the program. Out-dated and broken jewelry will do if necessary. Get a lot of pieces for the best effect.

Scripture:

"And they shall be mine, saith the Lord of hosts, in that day when I make up my jewels; and I will spare them, as a man spareth his own son that serveth him" (Mal. 3:17).

"There is gold, and a multitude of rubies: but the lips of knowledge are a precious jewel" (Prov. 20:15).

"As a jewel of gold in a swine's snout, so is a fair woman which is without discretion" (Prov. 11:22).

LEAD-UP MATERIAL:

Jewels[1]

When he cometh, when he cometh
 To make up his jewels,
All his jewels, precious jewels,
 His loved and his own.

He will gather, he will gather
 The gems for his kingdom,
All the pure ones, all the bright ones,
 His loved and his own.

Little children, little children
 Who love their Redeemer,
Are the jewels, precious jewels,
 His loved and his own.

Like the stars of the morning,
 His bright crown adorning,
They shall shine in their beauty,
 Bright gems for his crown.

REV. W. O. CUSHING

CHARGE:

In this jewel box I have lovely jewels representing the work of our new officers.

---

1. W. O. Cushing, "Jewels," from an old songbook published by the John Church Company in 1902.

It is a distinct honor to be chosen a jewel to serve your class this year. It is a privilege to be able to shine for Christ and magnify his church.

Will the *president* come to the front and be adorned with a jewel? (*Place some jewel from box on the president's dress.*) This jewel will shine and send forth glitter only as far as you have vision for the growth of the class. I will call your jewel the jewel of "Ideals." You are to lift up a common goal for all to follow.

Vice-president, come forward. (*Place on her a long string of beads*). You will wear the beads of "Stability." You are to be ready to help perform all necessary services. You will be the jewel that binds one to duty.

Will the *secretary* come to the front? I will adorn you with a jewel called "Benefit." All will benefit from your accuracy and patience. Your jewel will shine brightly as you read the minutes each time.

Treasurer, come and receive your jewels. The earscrews are always displayed so they can be seen by all. So your reports on the finances will be open to inspection at all times. We will call your jewels "Reality."

Will all the group leaders come together? (*Place on the group leaders a lot of jewelry—so much that they will look funny.*)

Your jewels are called "Work." If you fail to shine in your work with your groups, the whole class will suffer and fall behind. One jewel will be needed to work with some group members, and different jewels for others, for all have some problems.

Will any officers I have not called come to the front and receive a jewel of "Activity"? There are many ways to serve and all are important.

DEDICATION:

God's Will for You and Me

Just to be tender, just to be true,
Just to be glad the whole day through,
Just to be merciful, just to be mild,
Just to be trustful as a child,
Just to be gentle and kind and sweet,
Just to be helpful with willing feet,
Just to be cheery when things go wrong,
Just to drive sadness away with a song,
Whether the hour is dark or bright,
Just to be loyal to God and right,
Just to believe that God knows best,
Just in his promises ever to rest—
Just to let love be our daily key,
That is God's will for you and me.

(AUTHOR UNKNOWN)

"And they shall be mine . . . in that day when I make up my jewels" (Mal. 3:17).

THE DISTINGUISHED CROSS

BEST USE:

Can be adapted to almost any religious group.

EQUIPMENT NEEDED:

Place a white background on a flannel board or a poster. About the center of the board, place three black crosses. Let the center cross be larger. Prepare a halo with glitter on it. About midway of the lead-up material, place the halo above the center cross to make it a distinguished cross.

Before you finish talking, preferably as you mention each officer, place a figure of a kneeling person at the foot of the cross. One figure can be used for a pattern and as many as needed be cut out of black construction paper.

SCRIPTURE:

"Then said Jesus unto his disciples, If any man will come after me, let him deny himself, and take up his cross, and follow me" (Matt. 16:24).

"He that taketh not his cross, and followeth after me is not worthy of me" (Matt. 10:38).

LEAD-UP MATERIAL:

The Heart That Was Broken for Me

There came from the skies
  In the days long ago,
The Lord with a message of love;
  The world knew him not;
He was treated with scorn—
  This wonderful gift from above.

They crowned him with thorns,
  He was beaten with stripes,
He was smitten and nailed to the tree,
  But the pain in his heart
Was the hardest to bear,
  The heart that was broken for me.

He came to His own,
  To the ones that he loved,
The sheep that had wandered astray;
  They heard not his voice,
But the friend of mankind
  Was hated and driven away.

The birds have their nests,
  And the foxes have holes,
But he had no place for his head;
  A pallet of stone on the cold mountainside
Was all that he had for his bed.

(AUTHOR UNKNOWN)

(*At this point have a soloist sing "The Old Rugged Cross."*)
The cross has the power of attracting people. It draws out the best in men, in service and love.

The distinguished cross is a cross which foretells the kingdom of heaven. The distinguished cross reveals the opening of true paradise.

The distinguished cross leads to the commitment of followers to service.

CHARGE TO ALL OFFICERS:

Will all officers stand and by so doing pledge to serve to the best of your strength and ability during your term of service?

Lord, I Believe

Lord, I believe:
>That Jesus on Calvary died for my soul;
>That he is still seeking to make lost men whole,
>And heaven is longing to be our sure goal.
>>Lord, I believe.

Lord, I believe:
>That mine is a mission to tell to lost men
>The story of Jesus again and again,
>That, if they will trust him, he'll save them
>>from sin.
>>Lord, I believe.

Lord, I believe:
>Uphold me dear Saviour as onward I go;
>Give strength, that to sin, I may always say no,
>And help me win victory over the foe.
>>Lord, I believe.

J. T. BOLDING